# The Strategic Management Blueprint

## Paul Dobson and Ken Starkey

BLACKWELL
*Business*

First published 1993
Reprinted 1993

Blackwell Publishers
108 Cowley Road
Oxford OX4 1JF
UK

238 Main Street
Cambridge, Massachusetts 02142
USA

*British Library Cataloguing in Publication Data*
A CIP catalogue record for this book is available from the British Library.

*Library of Congress Cataloging-in-Publication Data*
Dobson, Paul.
    The strategic management blueprint/Paul Dobson and Ken Starkey.
        p.   cm.
    Includes bibliographical references and index.
    ISBN 0–631–18624–7
    1. Strategic planning.   2. Organizational change.   3. Management.
    I. Starkey, Ken, 1948–   .  II. Title.
    HD30.28.D62   1993
    658.4'012–dc20                                    92-31273
                                                      CIP

Typeset by TecSet Ltd, Wallington, Surrey
Printed in Great Britain by TJ Press (Padstow) Limited

This book is printed on acid-free paper

# The Strategic Management Blueprint

# Business Blueprints

This series presents the latest developments and concepts in the key business disciplines in an accessible way. Each title concentrates on the most crucial subjects within its area and presents the critical issues in a format and style that helps managers to develop real business skills. Using short case studies and practical examples the *Business Blueprints* series shows practising managers and students of management how to apply current management theory and best practice.

The *Business Blueprints* series is unique in its merging of the latest developments and concepts in management thinking with actual applications of those concepts.

*Published*

**The Marketing Blueprint**
Christine T. Ennew

**The Strategic Management Blueprint**
Paul Dobson and Ken Starkey

**The Business Accounting and Finance Blueprint**
Ian R. Davidson and Chris A. Mallin

61802

# Contents

# List of figures

# List of tables

# List of exhibits

# Preface

This book is about strategic management, the search for long-term competitive advantage. It analyses the key elements in strategy – the relationship between the firm and its environment, strategic choice, the link between strategy and organization and the management of strategic change – and illustrates the strategic management process with a wide variety of practical examples.

In writing this book we have put forward the current issues and techniques in strategic management in the form of a self-contained course rather than as a summary style textbook. Our 'mission' has been to develop a textbook that moves beyond being simply descriptive, and we have instead adopted a more critical approach and attempted to be prescriptive or suggestive where possible.

The book, as with the others in the Blackwell Business Blueprints series, is directed at core issues of real concern and direct applicability to management. Consequently, we use a focused approach rather than seek to cover a wide set of issues but deal with them too lightly to be of real use to management or develop students' critical skills. Questions and exercises have been set throughout the text with the aim of reinforcing the reader's understanding of the key issues, and this is backed up by illustrations and examples taken from the business world. The end result (hopefully!) is a book that is accessible to the non-specialist or practising manager, while also being useful for the business studies or MBA student. The style is user-friendly and technical jargon is carefully explained.

The book is also suitable for short courses in strategic management. As a short-course package the sections should be easy to follow, with summaries to reiterate the main points followed by questions aimed at applying the principles and techniques to one's own business (or at least a business with which you are familiar) to develop strategic management skills. In this respect the text is primarily geared towards management in private sector profit-oriented business, though the framework and the key principles can be readily adapted to cater for managing public sector organizations with, say, social or budgetary objectives.

The material in the book is based on the content of our short courses, MBA and undergraduate modules at the University of Nottingham and we are most grateful for the responses and suggestions of those managers and students who have kindly (unwittingly?) acted as our guinea-pigs while being subjected to the material. Similarly, we would like to thank our colleagues in the School of Management and Finance for their useful and perceptive comments on various drafts of the book. However, ultimately we accept full credit (and, of course, the blame) for the contents!

Paul Dobson
Ken Starkey

# 1 Introduction: what is strategic management?

## Two approaches to strategy

The idea of strategy has received increasing attention in the management literature. The literature on strategy is now voluminous and strategic management texts grow ever larger to include all the relevant material. In this text our aim is not to cover the whole area of strategy – that would require yet another mammoth tome – but to present a clear, logical and succinct approach to the subject that will be of use to the practising manager. We do not attempt a summary of the field, rather we present what we see as a useful framework for analysing strategic problems based on our own experience of teaching the subject on a variety of courses and to a variety of audiences over the years. Our premise is that a firm needs a well-defined sense of its mission, its unique place in its environment and scope and direction of growth. Such a sense of mission defines the firm's strategy. A firm also needs an approach to management itself that will harness the internal energies of the organization to the realization of its mission.

Views of strategy fall into two camps. There are those who equate strategy with planning. According to this perspective, information is gathered, sifted and analysed, forecasts are made, senior managers reflect upon the work of the planning department and decide what is the best course for the organization. This is a top-down approach to strategy. Others have a less structured view of strategy as being more about the process of management. According to this second perspective, the key strategic issue is to put in place a system of management that will facilitate the capability of the organization to respond to an environment that is essentially unknowable, unpredictable and, therefore, not amenable to a planning approach. We will consider both these views in this text.

Our own view is that good strategic management actually encompasses elements of each perspective.

There is no one best way of strategy. The planning approach can work in a stable, predictable environment. Its critics argue that such environments are becoming increasingly scarce, events make the plan redundant, creativity is buried beneath the weight and protocols of planning and communication rules. Furthermore, those not involved in devising the plan are never committed to its implementation. The second approach emphasizes speed of reaction and flexibility to enable the organization to function best in an environment that is fast-changing and essentially unpredictable. The essence of strategy, according to this view, is adaptability and incrementalism. This approach has been criticized for failing to give an adequate sense of where the organization is going and what its mission is. Critics speak disparagingly of the 'mushroom' approach to management (place in a dark room, shovel manure/money on the seeds, close the door, wait for it to grow!).

## Elements of strategy

Definitions of strategy have their roots in military strategy, which defines itself in terms of drafting the plan of war, shaping individual campaigns and, within these, deciding on individual engagements (battles/ skirmishes) with the enemy. Strategy in this military sense is the art of war, or, more precisely, the art of the general – the key decision-maker. The analogy with business is that business too is on a war footing as competition becomes more and more fierce and survival more problematic. Companies and armies have much in common. They both, for example, pursue strategies of deterrence, offence, defence and alliance. One can think of a well-developed business strategy in terms of probing opponents' weaknesses; withdrawing to consider how to act given this knowledge of the opposition generated by this probing; forcing opponents to stretch their resources; concentrating one's own resources to attack an opponent's exposed position; overwhelming selected markets or market segments; establishing a leadership position of dominance in certain markets; then regrouping one's resources, deciding where to make the next thrust; then expanding from the base thus created to dominate a broader area.

Strategic thinking has been much influenced by military thinking about 'the strategy hierarchy' of goals, policies and programmes. Strategy itself sets the agenda for future action, strategic goals state what is to be achieved and when (but not how), policies set the guidelines and limits for permissible action in pursuit of the strategic goals, and programmes specify the step-by-step sequence of actions necessary to achieve major objectives and the timetable against which progress can be measured. A well-defined strategy integrates an organization's major plans, objectives, policies and programmes and commitments into a cohesive whole. It marshals and allocates limited resources in the best way, which is defined by an analysis of a firm's unique strengths and weaknesses and of opportunities and threats in the environment. It considers how to deal with the potential actions of intelligent opponents.

Management is defined both in terms of its function as those activities that serve to ensure that the basic objectives of the enterprise, as set by the strategy, are achieved, and as a group of senior employees responsible for performing this function. Managers, in Sir John Harvey-Jones's phrase, are responsible for 'making it happen'. Our working definition of strategic management is as follows: all that is necessary to position the firm a way that will assure its long-term survival in a competitive environment. A strategy is an organization's way of saying how it creates unique value and thus attracts the custom that is its life-blood.

To understand the strategy of a particular firm we have to understand, unless we are in a start-up situation, what factors have made the firm what it is today. This involves answering questions such as: How did the organization reach its present state? Why is it producing its particular range of products and services? What kind of products or services does it intend to produce in the future, the same or different, and if different, how different? If it is thinking of altering its current range, what are the reasons for this? Strategy usually reflects the thinking of a small group of senior individuals, or even one strong leader, the strategic apex of a company. Why are the people who make up the strategic apex in this position? How do they think? Are there other (more) fertile sources of strategic thinking elsewhere in the organization that could be usefully tapped? If necessary how can one go about learning from the 'collective wit' of the organization, the creative voice that so often remains silent? How are decisions made in the organization? What is its management style, top-down or bottom-up, autocratic or democratic? Why is the organization structured in a particular way? What is the link between strategy and structure?

---

**Task**

Apply these questions to your own organization. (We will return to them later!)

---

## Our model of strategy

Our working model of the strategic management process is set out in figure 1.1. This is a model that works for us in terms of organizing our thinking about strategy and our attempts to understand the strategic issues facing particular firms. We do not suggest that this is the only model that is useful or that this is the best. (We just think it is!) Hopefully, in the course of your

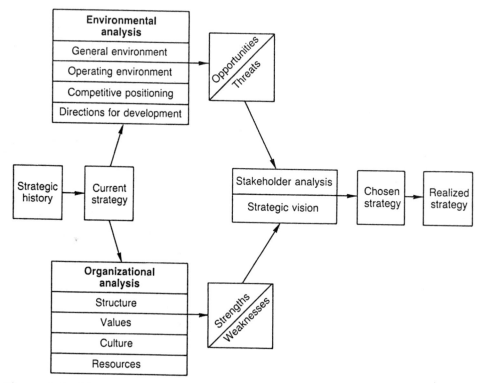

**Figure 1.1** The strategic management process

reading of this text and other work on the subject you will be critically analysing the various models suggested and the concepts upon which they rest. You may come to this text with your own model, developed out of your own experience. We suggest that you try working with our model and examine the extent to which it complements or contradicts your own and others. The result of such a critical appraisal will be a model with which you are comfortable and find useful in practice. If you feel that the model you develop is far superior to our own, please tell us about it! Remember, there is no one best answer in strategic management. If a firm chooses a particular strategic direction and it works in the way that very successful firms like IBM or, on a smaller scale, Body Shop have, the fact that it is successful does not mean that the choice of strategy was optimal, that it was the best. Another strategic decision might have led to even greater success. Conversely, if a firm makes a choice that leads to disaster, this does not necessarily mean that it could have made a better choice (though, with better decision-making, it hopefully could have done). The environmental conditions in its industry might have been such that this was the best choice, but that no choice, given its size or history, or the power of its competitors, could have changed its fate.

We will now explain our model, which provides the basis for subsequent chapters. *Current strategy* (italics indicates terms in the model) has its roots in the *strategic history* of a firm and its management and employees. We mention both management and employees here because, though in many cases senior management is the source of strategic decisions, it is the employees at the point of production or delivery of a product or service who are responsible for the actual implementation of a strategy. (Of course, in the final analysis it is management who are ultimately responsible for the performance of employees.) *Current strategy* is the result of the interaction of *intended strategy* and *emergent strategy*. The organization's actual strategy (its *realized strategy*) can be the direct result of strategic planning, the deliberate formulation and implementation of a plan. More often it is the outcome of the adaptation of such a plan to *emergent* issues in the environment. In some cases actual strategy can be very different from the strategy as planned or the firm might not have a very clear plan in the first place. In such cases the strategy can be described as *emergent* in the sense that strategy emerges from an ongoing series (sometimes described as a pattern or stream) of decisions.

Managers can decide that they are happy with their current strategy. They can take this decision in two ways. In a proactive sense they can scan their environment and the potential for change within their own organization and decide that to carry on doing what they are doing and what they are good at is the best way to face the future. In a less active, and far less satisfactory, way they can proceed on the basis of tradition – 'This is the way we have always done it. It has worked so far. That's good enough for us' – or inertia. Or management might decide that change is necessary. Again this can come about in a variety of ways. They might scan their environment and decide that there are major changes occurring in their business world to which they have to adapt. Or they might decide, through internal analysis, that they have the capability to develop a new way of doing business that will redefine the nature of the business they are in. Another stimulus to change can be the new manager appointed to a senior position who wants to leave his or her mark on the company and changes strategy primarily for this self-centred reason.

If change is the order of the day, then two issues need to be addressed: *environmental (external) analysis* and *organizational (internal) analysis*. (Remember, this is the ideal way of proceeding. In practice, managers might adopt only a partial solution and analyse only external or internal factors.) For a change of strategy to work there must be an alignment between internal capability and external opportunity. This is described as 'strategic fit'. The ideal situation is where there is a fit between the environment, a business need arising out of that environment that is strongly felt by a firm that has the sense of purpose (*mission*) and a management *system* that enables it to respond to this need with a coherent and practicable strategy. The potential to act in this way depends upon managerial judgement, managerial skill to exploit windows of opportunity and management ability to motivate other employees to support and commit themselves to the firm's new strategic objectives.

The analysis of the environment can be segmented into four interactive elements. There is the issue of the firm's *general environment*, the broad environment comprising a mix of general factors such as social and political issues. Then there is the firm's *operating environment*, its more specific industry/business environment. What kind of industry is the firm competing in? What 'forces' make up its 'industry structure'? Having examined its business environment, the issue then arises: how is the firm to compete in its industry? What is to be the unique source of its *competitive positioning* that will give it an edge over its competitors? Will it go for a broad market position, competing on a variety of fronts, or will it look for niches? Will it compete on the basis of cost or on the basis of added value, differentiating its products and charging a premium? What is the range of *options* that managers have to choose from? How are they to prioritize between these options? Does the company have strategic vision, a strong sense of mission, a 'reason for being' that distinguishes it from others? If change is necessary, what is to be the firm's *direction for development*? Having identified the major forces affecting its environment, how is the firm to approach the future?

*Organizational analysis* can also be thought of as fourfold. How is the firm organized? What is the *structure* of the organization, who reports to whom, how are the tasks defined, divided and integrated? How do the management systems work, the processes that determine how the organization gets things done from day to day – for example, information systems, capital budgeting systems, performance measurement systems, quality systems? What do organizational members believe in, what are they trying to achieve, what motivates them, what do they *value*? What is the *culture* of the organization? What are the basic beliefs of organizational members? Do they have a shared set of beliefs about how to proceed, about where they are going, about how they should behave? We know, thanks to Peters and Waterman's *In Search of Excellence*, that the basic values, assumptions and ideologies (systems of belief) which guide and fashion behaviour in organizations have a crucial role to play in business success (or failure). What *resources* does the organization have at its disposal – for example, capital, technology, people?

Management's role is to try to 'fit' the analysis of externalities and internalities, to balance the organization's *strengths and weaknesses* in the light of environmental *opportunities and threats*. A concept that bridges internal and external analyses is that of *stakeholders*, the key groups whose legitimate interests have to be borne in mind when taking strategic decisions. These can be internal groups, such as managers themselves and employees, or the owners of the firm, shareholders. They can also be external groups: the stock market if it is a quoted company, banks, consumers, the government.

Senior management's task is to try and align the various interest groups in arriving at its *chosen strategy* in the light of the creation of an appropriate *strategic vision* for the organization. Increasingly important here is the issue of corporate responsibility, how the organization defines and acts upon its sense of responsibility to its stakeholders. The broad responsibility to society at large is important here in, for example, such areas as 'green' (ecological) issues. Sometimes the various interest groups might be at odds with each other and management will have to perform a delicate political balancing act between them.

Having chosen a strategy, there is then the issue of implementation – in Sir John Harvey-Jones's phrase, making it happen. Very few schemes go totally (or even approximately) according to plan. The business environment changes, new issues emerge, green ones, for example. Some demand to be taken on board so that in many, perhaps the majority of cases, emergent strategy asserts itself to the extent that the *realized strategy* differs markedly from the chosen/planned strategy. In time, the realized strategy becomes a part of the firm's strategic history . . . and the strategy process continues.

*Note: strategic management in the public sector and the not-for-profit company* Most of what we will say in this text concerns the business firm looking towards profit as the source of its survival. We would, however, contend that much of what we say can be applied to the public sector organization or the not-for-profit firm. Similar principles of internal and external analysis apply.

## The growth vector

Strategic management involves decisions concerning what a company might do, given the opportunities in its environment; what it can do, given the resources at its disposal; what it wants to do, given the personal values and aspirations of key decision-makers; and what it should do, given the ethical and legal context in which it is operating. A firm needs a well-defined sense of where they are going in the future and a firm concept of the business it is in. We can think of these in terms of the firm's 'product–market scope' and 'growth vector'. This specifies the particular products or services of the firm and the market(s) it is seeking to serve. A firm's 'growth vector' defines the direction in which the firm is moving with respect to its current product–market scope. The key components of the 'growth vector' are set out in figure 1.2. One qualification is necessary here. The use of the growth vector assumes that the firm is indeed growing. This is obviously not always the case, and strategic decision-making might therefore involve 'downsizing' and withdrawal from some areas of business.

The *growth vector* illustrates the key decisions concerning the directions in which a firm might choose to develop. *Market penetration* comes about when the firm chooses as its strategy to increase its market share for its present product markets. If the firm pursues product development it sets out to develop new products to complement or replace its current offerings while staying in the same markets. It retains its current *mission* in the sense of continuing to attempt to satisfy the same or related consumer needs. In *market development* the firm searches for new markets with its existing products. If a strategy of *diversification* is chosen, the firm has decided that

| Product Mission | Present | New |
|---|---|---|
| Present | Market penetration | Product development |
| New | Market development | Diversification |

**Figure 1.2** Product, mission and market choices
*Source*: Adapted from Ansoff (1965)

its current product range and market scope is no longer adequate, and it actively seeks to develop new kinds of products for new kinds of markets.

* Let us illustrate the growth vector with an example concerning product–market strategy options in retailing. A retailing firm might decide to consolidate its position in its current markets by going for increased market share, perhaps through increased advertising. It might choose to develop new markets, perhaps expanding geographically into other areas, or even overseas, but retaining its current product range. It might choose to develop new retail products but stay in the same line of business, for example, increase its product range in clothing. It might choose to redefine the nature of these products. For example, the running shoe market was radically altered and expanded by redefining running shoes as leisure items, not merely as sports equipment. Finally, the firm might choose to move into totally different areas of business, for example, into financial services as Marks & Spencer has done. The range of product–market strategy options in retailing is illustrated in figure 1.3.

Governing the choice between strategic options should be the notion of *competitive advantage*. The firm has to identify *unique* opportunities for itself in its chosen area(s). It has to identify particular characteristics within its

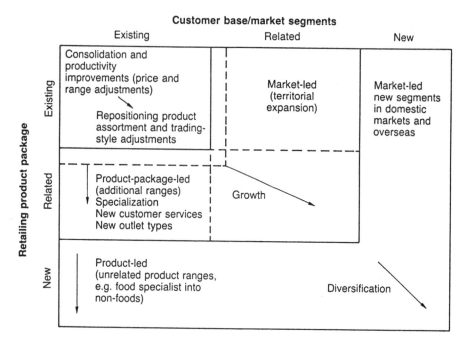

**Figure 1.3**   Retailing product–market strategy options
*Source*: Knee and Walters (1985)

approach to individual product–markets which will give it a strong competitive position. It might go for a large market share that will enable it to dominate particular markets and define the conditions of competition in them, for instance, as regards pricing policy. It might pursue technological dominance, looking for breakthrough products or a new manufacturing technology that will give it a technological edge over the competition, as Pilkington did, for example, with its development of the float glass process for manufacturing glass, which formed the foundation of the company's subsequent success. It might go for a better quality of product and service. In the automobile industry, Japanese manufacturers have rewritten the rules of the game regarding the quality of products and thus revolutionized consumer expectations. In the process they have made major inroads into Western markets historically dominated by Western firms. Or the firm might choose to combine some of these, as Sainsbury's has done with its 'good food' that 'costs less', an approach combining a low-cost advantage with a quality position in the world of supermarkets.

## Mission statements

The concept of mission has become increasingly fashionable in discussions of strategy. Indeed, some analysts go as far as asserting that a good 'mission statement' can provide an actual worthwhile alternative to the whole task of corporate planning. The definition of a firm's strategic *mission* encapsulated in the mission statement can be thought of as the first stage of the strategy process. Management guru Peter Drucker, the source of much contemporary thinking about the business mission, argues that asking the question 'What is our business?' is the same as asking the question 'What is our mission?' A business is defined by its mission. Only a clear definition of the mission of the organization makes possible clear and realistic business objectives, because the mission defines the purpose of the firm in terms of its enduring sense of its reason for being.

The mission defines the long-term vision of the organization in terms of what it wants to be and whom it wants to serve. A firm's mission should be clear and concise and distinguish it from any other firm. The mission statement has to be backed up with specific objectives and strategies, but these objectives and strategies are far more likely to be acted upon when there is a clear sense of mission informing action.

A good mission statement will contain the following:

- The purpose of the organization – a statement of the principal activities of a business or organization.
- Its principal business aims – its mission as regards the position it aims to achieve in its chosen business.
- The key beliefs and values of the company.
- Defininitions of who are the major stakeholders in the business.
- The guiding principles that define the code of conduct that tells employees how to behave.

Drucker illustrates the importance of a sense of mission with his story of three people working on a building site. All three were doing the same job but when asked what their job was gave very different answers. One answered 'Breaking rocks'; another answered 'Earning a living'; the third answered 'Helping to build a cathedral'. There is a similar story told about three climbers. When asked what they were doing, one answered 'Pitching camp'; the second answered 'Collecting material for a film'; the third answered 'Climbing Everest'. There are no prizes for deciding who was most committed to his/her task and who would be most motivated to perform to the best of his/her ability.

Drucker himself highlights the need to link a sense of mission to clear, achievable objectives. He makes the point when analysing the early success of Marks & Spencer:

> Marks & Spencer redefined its business as the subversion of the class structure of nineteenth century England by making available to the working and lower-middle-classes upper-class goods of better than upper-class quality, and yet at prices the working and lower-middle-class customer could well afford. . . . What made Marks & Spencer unique and successful . . . was its conversion of the definition of 'what our business is, and should be' into clear, specific, operationally effective and multiple objectives.   (Drucker, 1974: 96).

Figure 1.4 gives examples of some company missions.

---

## CASE STUDY

### Ford Motor Company
Figure 1.5 contains the mission statement of a leading multinational company, the Ford Motor Company.

Examine this statement and ask yourself the following questions:

1. Do you find it a satisfying statement of the company's mission?
2. Is there anything in the statement that you would wish to criticize?
3. Would you alter the statement in any way, either taking something out or adding more information to it?
4. What is the purpose of the mission statement for Ford?
5. Is it likely to fulfil this purpose?
6. The mission statement was devised by Ford in America. Is the very idea of a mission statement somehow inappropriate for the British context? Do the more reticent British, for example, feel uncomfortable with this kind of 'up-front' approach? Or is it equally useful in the United Kingdom and Europe? If you think it inappropriate, is there an alternative?
7. What would be an appropriate mission statement for your own firm or organization?
8. How are mission statements likely to differ in small and large firms?

---

'We are an international retailing group specialising in high technology consumer electronics, photography, office and home equipment and domestic appliances. We trade in the United Kingdom . . . and in the United States. . . . We aim to offer unrivalled value to our customers through the range and quality of the products we sell, the competitiveness of our prices and the high standards of in-store and after sales service we provide. . . ' – *Dixons Group*

'We are a precision engineering group internationally renowned for very high-speed processing applications in electronic, electrical and mechanical engineering. These skills are employed principally in the design, manufacture and marketing of machinery for the tobacco industry and for certain sectors of the packaging and printing industries. Our manufacturing operations are at sites in the UK and in the USA, Brazil, India and Australia. We maintain extensive research and development facilities in the UK and overseas. Our objective is to continue to design and manufacture machines which our customers regard as the best in the world.' – *Molins*

'Our aim is to *delight* our customers with *exceptional* products and *caring* service. Our goal is to be *widely* recognised as the *best specialist retailer* and *manufacturer* of quality confectionery . . . ' – *Thorntons*

' . . . we want satisfaction from accomplishments and friendships, balanced personal and professional lives, and to have fun in our endeavors . . . ' – *Levi Strauss*

'The strategy is to make our stores, our products and our people the very best in the business in the opinion of our customers . . . ' – *Tesco*

'[We] aim to be the world's leading chemical company, serving customers internationally through the innovative and responsible application of chemistry and related sciences . . . ' – *ICI*

'[Our] corporate purpose is the discovery, development, manufacture and marketing of safe, effective medicines of the highest quality . . . ' – *Glaxo*

'The NatWest way is to bring:
    QUALITY TO OUR CUSTOMERS . . .
    QUALITY TO OUR INVESTORS . . .
    QUALITY TO OUR PEOPLE . . .
    QUALITY TO OUR COMMUNITY . . . ' – *National Westminster Bank*

'Cadbury Schweppes . . . is a major international company with a clear focus on its two core businesses, confectionery and beverages . . . in more than 110 countries around the world.
    We are proud of the skills of our management and employees, which enable us to build upon our traditions of quality and value . . . ' – *Cadbury Schweppes*

**Figure 1.4**  Examples of company missions

## Mission

**Ford Motor Company** is a worldwide leader in automotive and automotive-related products and services as well as in new industries such as aerospace, communications, and financial services. Our mission is to improve continually our products and services to meet our customers' needs, allowing us to prosper as a business and to provide a reasonable return for our stockholders, the owners of our business.

## Values

How we accomplish our mission is as important as the mission itself. Fundamental to success for the Company are these basic values:

**People** – Our people are the source of our strength. They provide our corporate intelligence and determine our reputation and vitality. Involvement and teamwork are our core human values.

**Products** – Our products are the end result of our efforts, and they should be the best in serving customers worldwide. As our products are viewed, so are we viewed.

**Profits** – Profits are the ultimate measure of how efficiently we provide customers with the best products for their needs. Profits are required to survive and grow.

## Guiding Principles

**Quality comes first** – To achieve customer satisfaction, the quality of our products and services must be our number one priority.

**Customers are the focus of everything we do** – Our work must be done with our customers in mind, providing better products and services than our competition.

**Continuous improvement is essential to our success** – We must strive for excellence in everything we do: in our products, in their safety and value – and in our services, our human relations, our competitiveness, and our profitability.

**Employee involvement is our way of life** – We are a team. We must treat each other with trust and respect.

**Dealers and suppliers are our partners** – The Company must maintain mutually beneficial relationships with dealers, suppliers, and our other business associates.

**Integrity is never compromised** – The conduct of our Company worldwide must be pursued in a manner that is socially responsible and commands respect for its integrity and for its positive contributions to society. Our doors are open to men and women alike without discrimination and without regard to ethnic origin or personal beliefs.

**Figure 1.5**    The Ford Motor Company's mission, values and guiding principles

**Exhibit 1.1   Mission statements**

A recent study of mission statements in the United States argued that every organization should have one to motivate its employees. It claimed that firms with clear motivating mission statements were likely to perform better than those without. Classic mission statements cited include the Peter Drucker example of the men on the cathedral building site, President Kennedy's 'Put a man on the moon', Canon's 'Beat Xerox' and Komatsu's 'Encircle Caterpillar'. The trouble is that most mission statements tend to provoke cynicism and confusion rather than clarity and commitment by trying to combine statements of objectives with statements of values.

*Source*: adapted from *Financial Times*, 3 April 1989.

*Question*: Do you agree with the view expressed in exhibit 1.1?

There are four approaches to setting a mission (Collins and Porras, 1991):

- *Targeting* – setting a clear, definable target for the organization to aim at, such as the moon (the NASA moon mission statement!), financial/ growth targets or standards of excellence in product markets.
- *Focusing on a common enemy* – defeat of the common enemy guides strategic choice, e.g. Pepsi's 'Beat Coke', Honda's 'crush, squash, slaughter' Yamaha, Nike's attack on Adidas. Honda was so successful in its mission that Yamaha actually made a public apology for its claim that it would defeat Honda.
- *Role modelling* – sometimes used by smaller companies that model themselves on dominant players in their industry. In the computer industry IBM and Apple have provided, at least until recently, very different kinds of models.
- *Internal transformation* – used by older organizations faced with the need for radical change. This kind of mission has as its starting point the admission that its current mission is out of tune with the new realities it is facing.

*Question*: Which kind of mission do you think is best? Why?

## Strategy evaluation

Strategy can neither be formulated nor adjusted to changing circumstances without a process of strategy evaluation. Whether performed by an individual or as part of an organizational review procedure, strategy evaluation forms an essential step in the process of guiding an enterprise.

For many executives strategy evaluation is simply an appraisal of how well a business performs. Has it grown? Is the profit rate normal? If the answers to these questions are affirmative, it is argued that the firm's strategy must be sound. Despite its unassailable simplicity, this line of reasoning misses the whole point of strategy – that the critical factors determining the quality of current results are often not directly observable or simply measured, and that by the time strategic opportunities or threats do directly affect operating results, it may well be too late for an effective response. Thus, strategy evaluation is an attempt to look beyond the obvious facts regarding the short-term health of a business and appraise instead those more fundamental factors and trends that govern success in the chosen field of endeavour.

A strategy is a set of objectives, policies and plans that, taken together, define the scope of the enterprise and its approach to business. Rumelt suggests that three questions are central to the challenge of strategy evaluation:

1. Are the objectives of the business appropriate?
2. Are the major policies and plans appropriate?
3. Do the results obtained to date confirm or refute critical assumptions on which the strategy rests?

He further suggests that strategy must satisfy four broad criteria:

- *Consistency* – the strategy must not present mutually inconsistent goals and policies.
- *Consonance* – the strategy must represent an adaptive response to the external environment and to the critical changes occurring within it.
- *Advantage* – the strategy must provide for the creation and/or maintenance of a competitive advantage in the selected area of activity.
- *Feasibility* – the strategy must neither overtax available resources nor create unsolvable problems.

A strategy must be evaluated against each of these criteria; if it fails to meet one or more of them, the strategy is flawed. We will have more to say about strategy evaluation in the chapters that follow.

---

### Exhibit 1.2   Strategy

Inconsistency in strategy is not simply a flaw in logic. A key function of strategy is to provide coherence to organizational action. A clear and explicit concept of strategy can foster a climate of tacit coordination that is more efficient than most administrative mechanisms. Many high-technology firms, for example, face a basic strategic choice between offering high-cost products with high custom-engineering content and lower-cost products that are more standardized and sold at higher volume. If senior management does not enunciate a clear, consistent sense of where the corporation stands on these issues, there will be continuing conflict between sales, design, engineering and manufacturing people. A clear, consistent strategy, by contrast, allows a sales engineer to negotiate a contract with a minimum of coordination – the trade-offs are an explicit part of the firm's posture.

*Source*: Rumelt (1988).

---

## The text in brief

We divide the rest of the text into four sections. In chapters 2 and 3 we address the microeconomic aspects of strategic analysis, focusing on the structure of the firms's business environment, its internal resources and the range of strategic options open to it. In chapter 4 we turn to the management process aspects of strategy, looking first of all at organizational issues such as structure and culture. In the final chapter (chapter 5) we examine the issue of the management of strategic change. As in chapter 1 the text is interspersed with examples, illustrations and questions. We remind you here that every business strategy is unique: there is no 'one best way' of strategy. There is, therefore, no one right answer to the questions posed. The examples, illustrations and questions are meant to foster critical thought on the issues under discussion and to help you reflect critically on your own experience of strategy in action. Hopefully, you will finish the text a little closer to a 'model' of strategic management, a way of thinking about strategy with which you personally feel comfortable and able to discuss with others engaged in the same difficult but crucially important task of improving their understanding of strategic issues facing their businesses.

# 2 Situation analysis: the firm and its environment

## Introduction

In essence, the formulation of strategy is concerned with matching the capabilities of the organization with its environment. Situation analysis forms part of the background to which strategic decisions are made and provides insight into the difficulties of implementing strategic change. This chapter presents techniques for determining the firm's position in the environment. Applying these to one's own situation can help in identifying potential opportunities and threats facing the organization based on its strengths and weaknesses.

## *What do we mean by 'environment'?*

Figure 2.1 illustrates the organization in the context of various levels of its environment. The diagram represents the position of the organization relative to its external and internal environments – the greater the distance from the organization, the less direct effect there is on it. At the extreme the general environment concerns factors that not only affect the organization and its industry, but also the general business sector. More closely related to the organization is the operating environment, which is concerned with issues like the position of suppliers, buyers and competitors. At the centre of the diagram we see the internal environment with organization-specific factors.

While the diagram illustrates the degree to which different environmental factors affect the organization, conversely it also gives some indication of the extent to which the organization can affect (even manipulate) the environment by its behaviour and strategy. The environment should not simply be viewed as given (i.e. exogenous).

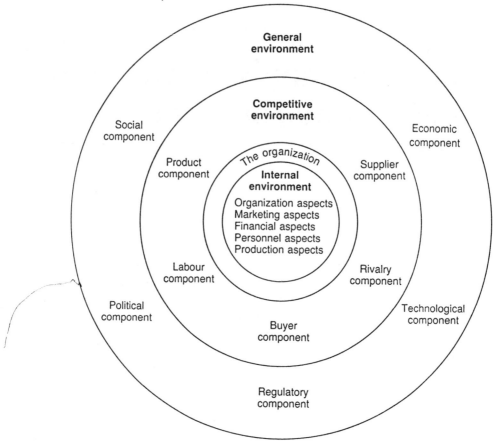

**Figure 2.1**   The organization and its environment

Rather the organization may be in a position deliberately to change the environment to its benefit – particularly the internal and the operating environment.

## How does one analyse the environment?

Figure 2.2 presents a six-step procedure for analysing the external and internal environment to identify the firm's strategic position (or standing):

1.  Undertake a general audit of environmental influences; the aim is to identify which of the many different sorts of general environmental factors have influenced the past performance and development of the organization along with some consideration as to which will in the future.

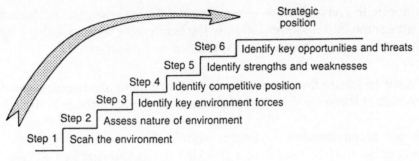

**Figure 2.2** Situation analysis

2.  Consider the nature of the organization's environment in terms of how uncertain it is. Is it (a) static/simple, (b) dynamic or (c) complex?
3.  Undertake a structural analysis to identify the key forces operating in the competitive environment.
4.  Analyse the organization's position relative to its competitors (either for resources or customers).
5.  Consider the internal environment with the aim of identifying the strengths and weaknesses of the organization.
6.  Undertake 'SWOT' (Strengths, Weaknesses, Opportunities and Threats) analysis where the understanding of the external environment (steps 1–4) is specifically related to the organization and its internal environment (step 5). This analysis is intended to identify opportunities and/or threats facing the organization and suggest how well positioned it is to meet these developments.

## Scanning the general environment

The first stage is to undertake a general audit of environmental influences affecting the organization. This involves the strategist 'sensing the environment', trying to get a general feel for which environmental forces are currently or in the future going to be more or less important to the organization. This process should be on-going and give initial indication of changes in the environment that may signal the need for changes in strategy. The process can throw up opportunities and warn of threats. Obviously different organizations will face different key forces. The intention is to consider how environmental forces affect the organization, and give some initial thought to how the firm might try to use these forces. The audit requires two related questions to be addressed:

- What factors in the general (wider) environment are affecting the firm?
- Which of these are the most important either presently or in the future?

Each set of environmental factors should be considered in turn. The following list may be useful as a checklist for identifying key forces:

1. Economic factors – (a) inflation, (b) unemployment, (c) disposable income, (d) business cycles, (e) interest rates, (f) GNP growth rates, (g) exchange rates, (h) energy and basic raw material prices.
2. Technological factors – (a) new discoveries/developments in own or related (e.g. supplier) industry, (b) speed of technology transfer (diffusion), (c) government spending on research, (d) rates of obsolescence.
3. Legal Factors – (a) employment law, (b) monopolies and mergers legislation, (c) environmental protection laws, (d) foreign trade regulations.
4. Political factors – (a) government stability, (b) taxation policy, (c) government spending, (d) government relations with other countries, (e) industrial policy (e.g. towards privatization, regulation and nationalization).
5. Social and cultural factors – (a) population demographics, (b) income distribution, (c) levels of education, (d) lifestyle changes, (e) attitudes to work and leisure, (f) consumerism, (g) social mobility.

Initially the scope should be broad. Once key changes have been identified, more detailed analysis should follow to determine the importance of the factor.

---

### Exercise

Identify the key forces in your organization's general environment. Which set of factors do consider to be most influential (a) at present, (b) in five years' time.

## The nature of the environment

Since strategic decisions are made in situations of uncertainty, the strategist must attempt to understand the nature of the environment facing the organization. By reducing the many environmental influences to a coherent pattern, strategic analysis aids understanding of the nature of uncertainty and provides guidance as to which methods are most appropriate for monitoring and evaluating strategic options.

The more dynamic (rapidly changing) or complex the environmental conditions are, the more uncertainty increases. Modern organizations are increasingly finding that they are facing both a dynamic and highly complex environment. Complexity comes in different forms. Firstly, it can result from the sheer diversity of environmental influences faced by an organization (e.g. multinationals). Secondly, it can arise because of the amount of knowledge required to handle environmental influences. Thirdly, it can be due to the different environmental influences which are, in themselves, interconnected (e.g. economic factors affecting and in turn being affected by technological, socio-cultural and political changes – particularly a problem for multinationals operating in the pharmaceutical, electronic, computer or automobile industries). Lowest uncertainty exists where the conditions are static and simple (e.g. raw material suppliers or in a traditional trade or profession, say a blacksmith or solicitor). Here technical progress is straightforward, competition may be limited and markets may be fixed over time. In these circumstances if change occurs it is likely to be fairly predictable.

Different methods are required for handling each type of environment.

*Simple/static environment*
Here the past acts as a good predictor of the future and thus environmental scanning is likely to be a more continuous and systematic exercise than in more dynamic situations where it is more intermittent. In a fairly static and simple situation it makes sense to undertake a detailed analysis of past environmental influences and use (quantitative) forecasting techniques to predict changes (with reasonable certainty).

*Dynamic environment*
The more the situation becomes dynamic, the less that can be learnt from past circumstances, and therefore focus should switch to considering the future and use of judgemental forecasting methods involving scenario planning. Here, the strategist constructs 'alternative futures', which

consider the likely behaviour of suppliers, competitors and consumers so that an overall picture of possible competitive environments can be built up. Strategic analysis can then be undertaken on each of the scenarios with different strategies developed for the different possible futures. Monitoring of the environment then provides the insight into which of the scenarios is likely to be most appropriate. There are, however, some potential problems with scenario (contingency) planning due to the risk of managers having myopic perceptions – since it is often difficult to conceive of markedly different scenarios and responses other than familiar ones.

Scenario planning is essentially a qualitative approach. It should involve detailed planning for at least three situations:

- the worst-case scenario (environment turns very unfriendly);
- the best-case scenario (where the operating and general environments are extremely favourable);
- the most likely case scenario (between the two extremes).

The analysis should show how the organization would respond to each scenario and formalize this in terms of *contingency plans*. (See exhibit 2.1.)

---

### Exhibit 2.1   Déjà vu: making the future feel familiar

In today's global and fast-changing environment, extrapolating from historical performance using medium- and long-term forecasting techniques has not proved very reliable. A number of companies, particularly big multinationals such as ICI and Pilkington, are replacing forecasts with a range of scenarios against which to test their plans for the future. One of the earliest converts was Royal Dutch/Shell, the world's most profitable company.

Traditionally, Shell planners would forecast refining plant requirements for several years ahead by extrapolating from current demand. However, the volatility in the oil market makes accurate prediction difficult. The following diagram shows how Shell underestimated oil demand in the 1950s and 1960s, and over-estimated it in the 1970s.

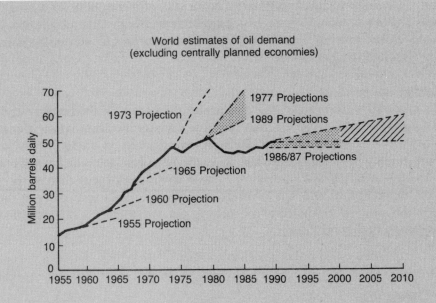

World estimates of oil demand
(excluding centrally planned economies)

Rather than relying on a single projection, Shell now develops a range of possible scenarios for managers to explore and imagine how they might act in differing conditions, so that when the future comes it 'feels' familiar. Forecasting is still used, but only to suggest possible scenarios – as seen in the 1980s projections.

According to Adam Kahane, head of socio-political, economic and technological planning for Shell International, 'scenarios alert you to what was previously invisible'. In his view this is very important since 'the ability to learn faster than your competitors may be a company's only sustainable competitive advantage'. The method proved particularly useful in the months around the Gulf War when the market was exceptionally volatile. When the war came, according to Mr Kahane there was little effect on Shell: 'None of our scenarios had involved such a violent clash, but we had considered a situation in which there was a serious disruption to oil supplies in the Gulf. Whether this came by war, or accident, or by religious fundamentalism did not really matter to us as the net effect is the same.'

*Source*: Adapted from 'Scenarios make the future feel familiar', *Independent on Sunday*, 24 March 1991.

The organization must regularly scan the environment, checking for signals that suggest the onset of a particular scenario. This monitoring acts as an early warning device so that the appropriate strategies can be implemented in good time.

*Complex environment*

In a complex environment the aim is simply to reduce the complexity! At the organizational level this may involve divisionalization when diversity is a problem, enabling each division/department to focus on its own environment. Structural analysis can involve sophisticated techniques such as model-building and simulation. These techniques focus directly on the key influences and attempt to model the interrelationships between them, with the aim of simulating the effects on an organization of different environmental conditions.

---

### Questions

1. How would you categorize your organization's environment?
2. Consider the conditions that (plausibly) describe your firm's worst-case scenario and best-case scenario. What probability do you assign to likelihood of them arising? (Are you worried?)
3. If your organization is one that operates in a complex environment, what measures would you propose to reduce this complexity?

---

## Structural analysis of the competitive environment

The third stage in analysing the environment is to place all the key influences and their degree of relevance within a framework of analysis which provides a structure to gauge the nature and intensity of competition. The framework commonly adopted is Michael Porter's, as shown in figure 2.3. Professor Porter's (1979, 1980) framework is essentially a structured means of examining the competitive environment of an organization so as to provide a clear understanding of the forces at work. Note that 'competition' is taken not to mean just product (or resource) competition, rather it is the broader notion of 'competition for profits'. The framework is based on the view that forces facing the industry play a key

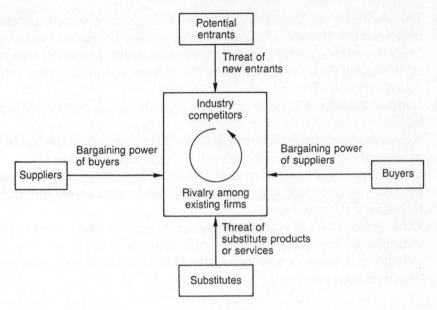

**Figure 2.3** The five forces of industry competition
*Source*: Porter (1980)

role in determining the profitability and success of an organization. Porter argues that 'the intensity of competition in an industry is neither a matter of coincidence nor bad luck. Rather it is rooted in its underlying structure' (1980). Understanding the industry structure and how the forces operate can aid performance if the organization can take action to avoid them or influence them. Then the task of the strategist is to determine which of the forces are of greatest importance to the organization and which can be influenced by the strategic decisions of the management.

There are five key forces to be considered:

*1 Entry barriers – how easy is it for a new firm to enter the industry?*
New entry into the industry invariably reduces the existing firms' profitability. Therefore, existing firms should be concerned with how easy it is to entry the industry. High entry barriers are generally required to maintain high industry profits. When possible, firms should seek to prevent (deter) new entry.

The following conditions make entry difficult:

(a) Significant economies of scale. (What is minimum efficient size and what are the consequences of operating below this level?)

(b) The industry is characterized by a high degree of product differentiation (either technical or perceived, say through advertising).

(c) There are high switching costs. (Are buyers and/or suppliers 'locked in' to dealing with the existing firms? Are there significant costs if they decide to switch?)

(d) Capital requirements for entry are high. (Are initial investment costs high?)

(e) Access to distribution is blocked. (New firms often face this problem in vertically integrated industries, e.g. petroleum, brewing.)

(f) Established firms have (absolute) cost advantages over a new entrant, e.g. due to the learning (experience) curve, access to inputs, or technological know-how).

(g) Existing firms would retaliate aggressively against a new entrant. (For example, a firm contemplating entry may be put off entering the industry if it believes that the existing firms would react with a price or advertising war.)

*2   Competitive rivalry – how intense is competition in the industry?*
The following are industry conditions usually associated with very intense rivalry and, in turn, low profitability:

(a) Slow growth. This can lead to a 'market share game' and result in intense price and non-price (especially advertising) competition.

(b) Large numbers of firms.

(c) High fixed costs. This creates pressure to use capacity, which encourages industry to overproduce, leading to lower prices.

(d) Lack of product differentiation. In this situation price is the chief weapon used in competition. In industries characterized by significant product differentiation (e.g. cars, cigarettes, computers) less aggressive forms of competition are used (e.g. advertising, research and development, quality differentiation).

(e) High exit barriers. If it is difficult to leave the industry, excess capacity may be a problem in the industry and result in low profitability. These exit barriers can be due to firms having specialized assets that they can sell, government intervention to maintain employment levels, or emotional barriers often associated with long-established family firms.

*3   Substitute products – what substitutes pose a threat to industry profitability?*
Pressure on an industry will be stronger the more close-substitutes (i.e. demand related) there are. In considering their influence, the strategist

needs to examine substitutes on their price-performance, their mark-ups and costs of production. Pressure will be greatest when:

(a) Firms producing substitutes are reducing costs (e.g. investing in new machinery).
(b) Substitute producers are increasing their demand by continued product innovation.
(c) Buyers switching costs are low (i.e. easy to transfer custom).
(d) There is intense competition between the substitute producers (leading to low prices and/or high levels of advertising).

4   *Power of buyers – how much bargaining power do buyers possess?*
Profit margins will be squeezed if the buyers have a strong bargaining hand. Buyer power is likely to be strong in the following situations:

(a) There are only a few buyers, each of which buys in large volume.
(b) Buyers can switch suppliers more easily than sellers can switch buyers.
(c) Buyers have full information on demand and costs.
(d) Buyers have the threat of integrating backwards.
(e) There are plenty of substitute products.
(f) Buyers are particularly sensitive to price, e.g. consumers, or buyers for whom the product purchase constitutes a large portion of its total costs.
(g) Quality is not important.
(h) Buyers profits are low and they therefore want to reduce costs.
(i) Buyers have selling influence, e.g. the power of retailers and wholesalers to promote a company's products by influencing consumers.

5   *Power of suppliers – how much bargaining power do suppliers possess?*
The points here are similar to those of buyer power. The power of suppliers is likely to be strong in the following circumstances:

(a) There are only a few suppliers. This may give them the power to dictate prices, quality and terms of trade.
(b) Highly differentiated inputs, e.g. good quality inputs giving buyers cost savings via improved efficiency.
(c) Lack of available substitute inputs.
(d) The industry is not an important customer of the supplier group.
(e) Cost relative to total purchases is high.

(e)  Suppliers have the threat of forward integration.
(f)  The workforce (which, of course, 'supplies' labour) is organized in a trade union.

The strength of these five forces will vary between industries, and consequently so do levels of industry profitability. As Porter (1980) puts it, the

> collective strength of these forces determines the ultimate profit potential in the industry. . . . The forces range from intense in industries like tyres, paper and steel – where no firms earn spectacular returns – to relatively mild in industries like oil-field equipment and services, cosmetics, and toiletries – where high returns are quite common.

Exhibit 2.2 shows a structural analysis of the UK carbonated soft drinks industry, examining the impact the various forces have on this industry. This exhibit highlights the competitive significance of the power of retail grocery chains. The intensity of competition within the industry is quite high, with regular advertising wars taking place; on the other hand sales are increasing and the products are (perceived as) differentiated. On the plus side there are quite high barriers to entry due to the high capital requirements required for production and distribution, increasingly advanced and specialized technology, lack of access to distribution, and strong consumer loyalty to recognized brands.

---

**Exhibit 2.2   Structural analysis of the UK carbonated soft drinks industry**

Background

Carbonated soft drinks in the United Kingdom account for 10 per cent of all beverages consumed and 50 per cent of the soft drinks market. The carbonated soft drinks market is worth over £3bn at retail prices, with annual output exceeding 4bn litres. The products are distributed to around 300,000 outlets.

Around 125 firms operate in the industry, directly employing some 23,000 workers. However, two companies, Coca-Cola and Schweppes Beverages and Britvic Soft Drinks, dominate the industry with 40 and 22 per cent of the market (by volume) respectively. Only three other companies, A. G. Barr, Carters and Wells, have more than 3 per cent of the market. The industry is currently being investigated by the Monopolies and Mergers Commission (which is due to report in 1992).

## 1   Threat of entry

Entry into the market on a large scale is difficult. The major companies have essentially tied up the distribution channels in grocers and public houses. Furthermore, because the products are 'experience' goods, and reputation matters, very heavy advertising would be a necessity to gain a foothold. Although there is the possibility that with the removal of trade barriers and harmonization in the European Community a major continental firm might plan an assault on the UK market, even so the current barriers to entry would still make this form of entry an extremely difficult task.

## 2   Threat of substitutes

There are a number of substitutes for carbonated soft drinks, e.g. tea, coffee, beer (especially low or non-alcoholic), wine and other alcoholic beverages. However, carbonates have been gaining share at their expense and this trend is likely to continue; the threat posed is thus relatively weak.

## 3   Power of suppliers

Again, relatively weak pressure with the exception of sugar producers and plastic suppliers (e.g. Du Pont). The workforce is not highly organized nor is it militant.

## 4   Power of buyers

Over 50 per cent of sales are sold through grocers. The top five grocery chains account for over 60 per cent (and increasing) of all grocery sales and are thus in a strong bargaining position. Some 12 per cent of sales are through public houses, which are in the main controlled by powerful brewers (though following the recent MMC report, the enforced sell-off of pubs is likely to weaken the position of the major brewers). The remainder of sales are to relatively weak buyers, including off-licenses, CTNs (confectioners, tobacconists and newsagents) and restaurants/cafeterias.

## 5   Competitive rivalry

Rivalry is intense, particularly between the two dominant companies. Rather than (damaging) price competition, the rivalry is usually in terms of very heavy advertising, which serves to increase the size of the market. Industry advertising expenditure in 1989 was £66.1m (two-thirds of all advertising on soft drinks). Competition is also in terms of the products themselves, with new segments continuously being developed. Again, this form of competition extends the size of the whole market. Segmentation and differentiation are key aspects in the market and particular firms dominate particular segments, lessening the intensity of competition overall.

### Conclusion

The strongest pressures come from the power of buyers and the fairly intense competition within the industry. Nevertheless, overall the industry looks to be in a fairly healthy position: the leading firms are very profitable and industry growth is expected to be maintained over the next four years at an annual rate of 8 per cent (by volume). Furthermore, the firms are actively competing on quality and bringing new products to the market, as well as being innovative in terms of reducing costs by investing in new technology and machinery, developing new forms of packaging and offering better distribution services.

*Source*: MBA research project at the University of Nottingham.

---

**Exercise**

Consider the key pressures facing your industry (both currently and in the near future). Rank order (1–5) each category from the most to the least significant. State your reasons for this choice.

---

## Identifying the firm's competitive position

Step 4 in environmental analysis is to identify the organization's competitive position. The first exercise might be to compare the effect environmental influences (identified by the audit) have on the firm and its main competitors. Exhibit 2.3 is a competitive assessment of the major grocery chains in terms of changes in consumer profiles. It assesses the overall impact the changes are likely to have on the companies. Overall they appear to be in a reasonably good position to meet the changes.

## Exhibit 2.3 Competitive standing of major grocery chains in relation to changing consumer profiles

| Grocers | Increasing affluence | 'Two nations' (N–S divide) | Car ownership | Healthy living | Price Conscious-ness | Snacking/ prepared meals | Overall impact |
|---|---|---|---|---|---|---|---|
| Sainsbury's | + + + Excellent quality perception | + Good exposure in south | + + + Large sites; good positions | + + + Highly innovative | + + 'Good food cost less'; own-brands | + + Good range | + + + Excellent |
| Tesco | + + Good quality perception | 0 Neutral | + + Moving to out-of-town sites | + + Good perception | + + Good | + + Good | + + Good |
| Argyll (Safeway Lo'cost) | + Fair | 0 | + + Good | + Fair | + + Good | + Fair | +/+ + Fair to good |
| Asda | + + Good quality perception | – Exposure in north | + + + Excellent large sites | + + Good perception | + + Good | + + Good | + + Good |
| Gateway | + Fair | 0 | + + Moving to large sites | + Fair | + Fair | + Fair | + Fair |
| KwikSave | 0 Operates at bottom end of market | 0 | + Fairly small sites | 0 | + + + Excellent | 0 | + Fair |
| Co-op | + Fair | 0 | + Mixture of sites | 0 | + Fair | + Fair | 0 / + Relatively weak |
| Marks & Spencer | + + + Excellent; top quality perception | 0 | 0 Mostly inner town sites but some new developments | + + Good reputation | – Rather pricy foods | + + + Excellent range | + + Good |

Key:   + + +  =  excellent; + +  =  good; +  =  fair: 0  =  neutral; –  =  weak.

Such an exercise serves a useful introduction to understanding the positions of competitors. Beyond this the strategist requires a more thorough yardstick by which to gauge competition, and in turn the firm's position. We briefly outline three frameworks commonly used: the lifecycle model, strategic group analysis and market share (segmentation) analysis.

### The lifecycle model

This represents a relatively simple way of conceiving the firm's position in terms of the stage of development of its markets (i.e. their position in the lifecycle of such markets). The model is based on the view that conditions in the market place, in terms of growth and maturity of markets, fundamentally affect market conditions and competitive behaviour. Figure 2.4 summarizes some of the conditions that can be expected at

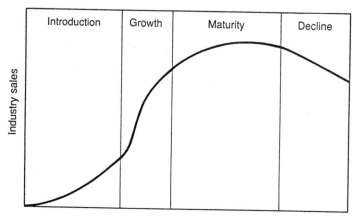

| | Introduction | Growth | Maturity | Decline |
|---|---|---|---|---|
| Growth rate | Rising slowly | Accelerating | Levelling | Declining |
| Sales | Low | Rising | Peak | Declining |
| Unit costs | High | Declining | Low | Low |
| Product line | Very short | Growing | Diversified | Shrinking |
| Profits | Negative | Increasing | High but declining | Declining |
| Competitors | Few | Increasing | More but stable | Declining |
| Typical pricing | Cost-plus | Penetration | Competitive | Cut |
| Entry barriers | Technology | Start-up costs | Competitors | Overcapacity |
| Typical advertising | Information and education | Mass-market awareness | Persuasion and differentiation | Reduced |

**Figure 2.4**   Stages in the lifecycle

different stages in the lifecycle. Generally, different strategies are required at different stages in the lifecycle to cope with the different competitive conditions. For instance, the nature of the game changes substantially when one moves from the growth phase, where firms develop independently, to the mature phase, where growth can only come about at the expense of rivals.

The model is designed to be of use in considering the lifecycle of a firm, but more often the lifecycle of the product(s) it produces. The picture is, of course, only a stylized representation. Some products may experience explosive growth then sudden collapse, e.g. fad items such as hula-hoops and Cabbage Patch Dolls. Meanwhile, other products may have very long stages of development (possibly over hundreds of years) and have yet to enter the decline phase, e.g. beer and wine. It is also possible that rather than entering the decline phase, some mature products can receive a sudden impetus due to further product differentiation and innovation, which leads to further industry growth – the so-called rejuvenation phase.

---

**Questions**

1. What stage of the lifecycle would you consider your company's main product/service to be in?
2. Consider possible courses of action that your company could reasonably take when its main product reaches the end cycle.

---

*Strategic group analysis*

The aim here is to focus on the group of firms that are the closest rivals to the organization. Rivalry can be defined in different terms (depending on the nature of the industry). The strategic group will generally share similar strategic characteristics, follow similar strategies and compete on similar bases.

It is usual to define groups using two sets of characteristics as a basis of competition. Exhibit 2.4 identifies strategic groups in the (worldwide) car industry, in this case in terms of the degree of corporate diversity and geographic coverage. When constructing such a map the characteristics should be chosen to show distinct groupings of firms (i.e. to differentiate groupings clearly) as well as key industry characteristics. The characteristics depend to a large extent on the history and development of the industry and the competitive forces at work in the industry.

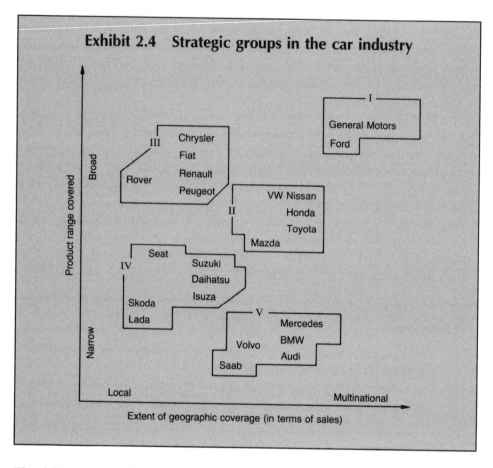

Exhibit 2.4 Strategic groups in the car industry

The following is a list of characteristics that might be considered:

(a) extent of product diversity;
(b) number of market segments covered;
(c) extent of vertical integration;
(d) size of organization;
(e) product quality;
(f) marketing effort (size of salesforce, budget or advertising spread);
(g) ownership structure (independent or owned by parent);
(h) R&D capability (extent of product or process innovation);
(i) extent of geographic coverage;
(j) pricing policy;
(k) extent of product branding;
(l) perceived value of product (price/quality).

As well as giving a good understanding of the competitive characteristics of competitors, this form of analysis allows one to ask how likely or possible it is to move from one strategic group to another. For example, in the car industry (exhibit 2.4), firms in group III, though they have broad product ranges, have yet to break away from a large dependence on their local market. Capital requirements, lack of distribution networks and the decision to produce domestically have prevented them from becoming truly multinational. On the other hand, the industry's giants in group I find it difficult to compete at the high end of the market against the specialized firms in group V, which have the advantages of consumer loyalty (snobbery?), experience, highly focused research and development, and, particularly because cars are 'experience' goods, reputation for quality. (Although in Ford's case this has to an extent been circumvented by the takeover of Jaguar.)

---

**Question**

Do you consider the groupings identified in exhibit 2.4 to be reasonable? Consider other combinations of characteristics. Do other groupings emerge?

---

**Exercise**

Construct two strategic group maps for your own industry. Which is the more useful of these maps for strategic considerations? Having identified the most appropriate groupings, give a brief assessment of how easy it is for a firm to enter your group and how easy it is for your organization to move to another group.

---

*Market share analysis*

It is widely held, and with some justification, that market share is a measure of market power. A high market share bestows benefits to a firm in the form of reduced costs due to economies of scale, buying power and experience. A firm's position relative to its competitors should then be viewed in terms of its market share in the market as a whole and also its share in the various segments of the market.

Market share analysis attempts to map out the relative power of competitors according to shares held in market segments. This should help the strategist identify where its strengths and weaknesses lie. Breaking the market into segments should also help in identifying opportunities open to the firm (and its competitors!), and may give further insight into the strategies that competitors are following.

A market can be segmented in various ways. The strategist may want to experiment with different classifications, since each basis could give rise to a different assessment of environmental opportunities. Having identified the segments, the relative sizes (in percentage terms) and likely growth then need to be estimated and the market segment position of each firm (in terms of rankings or 'weak, middling, dominant') for each segment identified. As with strategic group analysis, the basis of segmentation should hopefully discriminate between the firms. The firm's overall position is assessed in terms of the intensity of competition it faces in its main market segments and how difficult it is expand or to move into growing and/or profitable segments.

---

### Exercise

1. Consider different classifications of segments for your industry. Which classification appears to be most appropriate? Why?
2. Identify those segments that your firm is dominant in and particularly weak in.
3. Which segments are rapidly growing and/or highly profitable? Are rivals in a stronger position to exploit these? If yes, what do you think your company should do?

---

## The internal environment: resources and capabilities

Having gained an understanding of the external environment facing the firm, the next stage is to assess the firm's resources with the intention of identifying its strategic capability based on understanding its strengths and weaknesses. This should then provide guidance for assessing the suitability

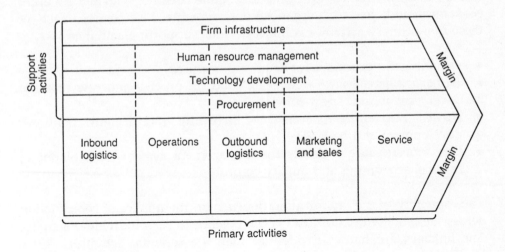

**Figure 2.5**   The value chain
*Source*: Porter (1985)

of particular strategies (i.e. can they be sustained?) as well as for resource planning and deployment.

The capability of any organization is fundamentally determined by how well it links together its various activities – such as designing, marketing, delivering, and supporting its products and services. Figure 2.5 shows how activities are linked together to form the *value chain*. Here the amount of value added, rather than costs, are assigned to each activity. Value chain analysis considers where and how a firm adds value (i.e. the internal factors that drive profitability). The diagram represents the linkages between 'primary' activities and the 'supporting' activities. The primary (i.e. the main value-adding) activities are grouped into five main areas:

- *Inbound logistics* – concerned with receiving, storing, and distributing inputs.
- *Operations* – transforming the inputs into the final product/service.
- *Outbound logistics* – moving the product to buyers (including warehousing and distribution).
- *Marketing and sales* – bringing the product to buyers and inducing them to buy and use it.
- *Service* – activities to enhance or maintain the value of the product/service (including installation, repairs, maintenance, training and other services).

The primary activities are generally quite distinct, having different economies and, in large organizations, separate cost centres. Each of these five primary activities is linked to four supporting activities:

- *Procurement* – processes for acquiring resources.
- *Technology development* – covering product, process and raw material development and 'know-how'.
- *Human resource management* – including recruitment, training, development and rewards.
- *Firm infrastructure* – chiefly the management systems, e.g. planning, finance, accounting and quality control.

The capability of the organization depends on the quality of coordination across these activities, not just on competence in each individual activity. The linkages are harder to identify than the separate activities. Porter (1985) defines such linkages as 'relationships between the way one activity is performed and the cost and performance of another'. A good example is provided by just-in-time production, where parts procurement and assembly are tightly linked. It is often such linkages that provide competitive advantage. Building further linkages will increase value added. This provides a further mechanism to differentiate your company from its competitors.

To determine the firm's internal position we then need to assess these activities, which in turn depend on the resources at hand in the organization. The process begins with an audit of the firm's resources. This should enable management to decide on how well the resources are being utilized – i.e. how efficiently and effectively they are being used and how well they are being controlled. This analysis, in the context of the firm's activities, will hopefully identify the company's key strengths (i.e. good attributes) as well as identify missing or 'poor' resources that need to be attended to.

The following resources should be considered:

- *Physical resources* These include buildings, materials, production facilities, production techniques, information system, distribution network, research facilities. Efficiency will concern capacity fill, unit costs, yield, layout and materials flow. Effectiveness should be measured by the match between the various resources.
- *Human resources* This is in terms of the number of employees, their productivity (set against wages and salaries), the extent and balance of technical and other skills (also competence, versatility, flexibility),

knowledge (awareness), experience, attitudes (degree of interest and effort, team spirit, management style), and their demographic characteristics (age structure).

- *Financial resources* The financial capability depends on factors like financial size, growth pattern, profitability, use of working capital, price–earnings ratio, asset structure and capital structure. The analyst will need to assess the costing system, budgets and investment appraisal procedures.
- *Intangibles* This category is especially important for firms in the service sector where value depends on 'goodwill' arising from brand names, company image, reputation, good contacts, etc. Effectiveness depends on how well this exploited, e.g. by public relations.

Assessing the resources and activities of the firm relies on various criteria, most notably:

1. historical experience;
2. competitors and other comparable firms ('industry or business norms');
3. personal opinions (involving value judgements) of management and consultants;
4. specific targets accomplished, e.g. budgets.

The assessment of the individual resources and activities then forms the background to judging the organization as a whole. This process should take into account the efficiency and effectiveness of the organization's form and structure, its standard operating procedures, the control system, the planning system and top management.

'But where does one obtain the information?' we hear you cry! The following should prove to be the most useful:

- personal observation and experience;
- customer contacts;
- accounts and planning and control system documents;
- managers, other employees, board members;
- competitive intelligence;
- consultants;
- published information (books, journals, magazines, newspapers).

The main problem will not be lack of data; rather it will concern turning all the quantitative (especially the financial) measures into a meaningful (i.e. comprehensible) qualitative assessment!

The end result of the analysis should be the identification of the key issues – the major strengths and weaknesses – and their strategic importance. In terms of developing suitable competitive strategies the analysis should identify the areas where the firm has 'distinctive competence', arising from its strengths, giving it an edge over its rivals and give guidance where particular weaknesses are to be avoided.

In considering the core competence of the organization one should not forget the links with external parties which provide key services to the organization, as these links can provide a useful source of competitive advantage if they are successfully organized and controlled. The firm should examine whether these business services are more usefully carried out externally to the organization (i.e. contracted out) or should be 'internalized' and carried out within the organization (i.e. performed 'in-house'). Even for manufacturing firms the range of business services used can now be extensive and service activities are important at all stages of the value chain. Many companies choose to contract out some services that could be handled equally well in-house so that they can focus on the core business. These services would now typically include building main-tenance services, order processing, payroll processing and direct market-ing, among others, where 'dedicated' service providers may be able to provide superior services at a lower cost simply through specialization – in terms of both personnel and technology. As Porter (1990) argues, the drive to de-integrate business services appears to be growing (with the exception of legal services). The reason for this is the increasing capital intensity of service firms, which were traditionally extremely labour intensive. Information technology and the use of computers and computerized techniques have revolutionized the manner in which functions are undertaken, leading to better control operations and increased employee productivity. The once highly fragmented service sector is now rapidly consolidating and an increasing number of large, even international, companies are emerging (e.g. Saatchi & Saatchi in advertising). The advantage of using the specialized service firm over an in-house unit is essentially twofold. Firstly the specialist provider faces competition for the account and has the incentive to raise productivity and quality while keeping costs down. The (captive) in-house service department, on the other hand, is a cost-centre and does not face such competitive pressures to ensure that productivity and quality is optimum. Secondly, the service provider, being specialized and concentrating its efforts, can often hire and train people more effectively, employ better methods, use more up-to-date equipment, and perform the service cheaper and better. Meanwhile, the in-house service department may be regarded as of peripheral concern to the core activities of the business and lack the necessary flexibility if it is constrained to the guidelines of the other functions of the organization. This ultimately leads to an inefficient and ineffective service compared to what could be provided by an independent firm.

The one potential disadvantage with using outside service providers concerns communication and thus effective control. The development of large, specialist firms has, however, led to a more professional relationship with clients, and technology has allowed communication to become more instantaneous. The difficulties of dealing with outside service suppliers have thus been significantly reduced. Indeed for many firms the links with outside suppliers, where a high level of cooperation and coordination has been effected, are a chief source of competitive advantage over rivals.

## Questions

1. Consider how your firm assesses its capabilities. Is there a formal procedure for monitoring the internal environment?
2. Apply the concept of the value chain to your organization. Which is your (a) strongest and (b) weakest activity? Are there good links across the activities? Can you identify any room for improvement?
3. (a) Identify any activities the organization currently undertakes that could be more fruitfully contracted out to specialist service providers. (b) Similarly, identify any activities that would probably be better carried out by the organization, i.e. internalized.
4. The value chain approach is also extremely useful for comparing your own position against that of your rivals. Firms producing the same product or service for the same market will often have different competencies in and across the various activities, which results in the different competitive standings amongst the firms. Consider the internal environment of your main rivals. Which areas are they strong and weak in? What are their strengths and weaknesses? Does this suggest any opportunities and/or threats?

## 'SWOT' analysis

The final step in situation analysis is to determine the firm's strategic position by considering whether or not the present strategy of the firm is capable of dealing with the changes taking place in the business environment. The method typically used is SWOT analysis, which aims to relate the strengths and weaknesses of the organization (based on an internal audit of the firm's capabilities – see next chapter for more detail) against the opportunities and threats thrown up by the analysis of the external environment. In order to conduct this type of analysis the management must have a clear view of what the current strategy is. This is not always obvious!

Essentially one wants to identify opportunities and threats, while at the same time identifying key aspects of organizational capability that provide strengths and weakness in dealing with these environmental changes.

Opportunities and threats facing firms will not only differ across industries but also in the same industry. The following list gives some suggestions to help identify the main opportunities and threats facing a particular firm:

*Opportunities – these should be exploited!*
1. market share;
2. experience;
3. financial strength;
4. technological leadership;
5. good products (especially trade names);
6. low cost;
7. economies of scale;
8. distribution system;
9. skilled personnel;
10. favourable public image.

*Threats – these must be overcome by reviewing and appraising them realistically*
1. market saturation;
2. changes in consumer tastes;
3. demographic shifts;
4. shortages in factor-input supplies (including skilled labour);
5. economic uncertainty (inflation? recession?);
6. competitors' market power;
7. government regulations (including European Community);
8. pressure groups;
9. political uncertainty (change in the government?);
10. change in trade policy (breakdown of free trade agreement?).

Let us then look at a simple procedure for matching up the identified opportunities and threats against the strengths and weakness of the organization (which emerge from analysing the firm's internal environment). The following five-step procedure is adapted from Johnson and Scholes (1988):

1. Identify the current or prevailing strategy or strategies in the organization.
2. Identify the key changes in the firm's environment.
3. Identify the key capabilities (strengths) and key limitations (weaknesses) of the organization (i.e. consider its resources).
4. List the key environmental issues against the relevance of the current strategy and the strengths and weaknesses of the organization.
5. Then examine the statements against each other, and score either a + (or a weighted ++) or a − (or a − −) or 0, as follows:

   (a) Mark + if there would be a benefit to the organization, i.e. a strength that would enable the firm either to take advantage of, or counteract, a problem from an environmental change, or offset a weakness caused by the change.
   (b) Mark − if there would be an adverse effect on the firm, i.e. either a strength would be reduced by the change or a weakness would prevent the firm from overcoming the problems associated with an environmental change.
   (c) Score 0 if there is no (or only a minimal) effect.

Exhibit 2.5 is a completed SWOT analysis for a firm producing carbonated soft drinks. It shows that the major opportunities for the firm arise from the

**Exhibit 2.5   A SWOT analysis of a carbonated soft drinks producer**

| Key Issues in the environment | Restructuring of brewing industry | Growing industry sales | Consumer lifestyle changes (inc. dieting) | Competitors' market power | Environmental issue of packaging | Growing power of grocery chains | + | − |
|---|---|---|---|---|---|---|---|---|
| Current strategies | | | | | | | | |
| Develop brand leaders | + | + | 0 | + | 0 | +/− | 4 | 1 |
| Further backwards integration | 0 | + | 0 | 0 | + | +/− | 3 | 1 |
| Increase market share | + | 0 | 0 | − | + | − | 2 | 2 |
| Main strengths | | | | | | | | |
| Location of plant | + | + | 0 | + | 0 | 0 | 3 | 0 |
| Advanced product system | + | + | 0 | + | + | 0 | 4 | 0 |
| Good distribution service | + | + | 0 | + | 0 | + | 4 | 0 |
| Packaging innovation | 0 | + | 0 | + | + + | 0 | 4 | 0 |
| Financially sound | + | + | + | + | + | + | 6 | 0 |
| Main weaknesses | | | | | | | | |
| No strong brands | − | 0 | 0 | − − | 0 | − − | 0 | 5 |
| Dependence on own-label sales | − | 0 | 0 | − − | 0 | − − | 0 | 5 |
| Perceived low-quality products | − | | − | − − | 0 | − | 0 | 5 |
| No canning facility | 0 | + | − | − | − | − | 1 | 4 |
| No product range | 0 | − | 0 | − | 0 | − | 0 | 3 |
| + | 6 | 8 | 1 | 6 | 6 | 4 | | |
| − | 3 | 1 | 2 | 9 | 1 | 10 | | |

*Source*: Adapted from Johnson and Scholes (1988).

expected continued growth of sales and (because the company is at the forefront of research and development in packaging drinks) the environmental issue of packaging. To a lesser degree, the restructuring of the brewing industry with the release of tied public houses may give an opportunity to increase sales, though the lack of strong brands is likely to inhibit the company deriving much advantage. Threats are chiefly from the growing power of the grocery chains, where most of the firm's sales currently go to, and competitors' market power, which is likely to further squeeze margins and the firm's market share unless it can develop brand leaders.

The analysis, though crude, provides some rating of the opportunities and threats, as well as showing the degree to which current strategies address the issue of a changing environment. In this case showing the importance of developing brand leaders.

## Conclusion

Armed with a sound knowledge of the firm's environment the strategist can begin to contemplate strategic options. In evaluating these options SWOT analysis may prove useful as a simple ready-reckoner, though there are a number of other more sophisticated and specialized methods for evaluating options.

We end this chapter with two points to bear in mind. The first is the need for environmental/situation analysis to be viewed as a continuous process and not to be neglected. Sudden radical shifts in the broad or operating environments have been known to catch out leading players in a number of industries. In particular where there has been a major upheaval in an industry, especially through government intervention in deregulating the market, some firms are noticeably more able to cope with these changes than others. Exhibit 2.6 highlights some of the changes that occurred in the financial services sector when the industry underwent a radical change as a result of a short series of legislation in the late 1980s. This began an explosive chain of events that fundamentally altered the nature of the industry.

---

### Exhibit 2.6   Deregulation of the financial services market

Deregulation and liberalization of markets has been a common feature in recent times, not only in the United Kingdom under the Thatcher government of the 1980s, but also in other countries where the 'privatization bug' has caught on. Great changes have occurred both in terms of the opening-up of individual markets to encourage more competition, e.g. in the European Community and the United States, and the radical transformation of the former Communist countries in eastern Europe, where privatization has taken place across whole economies.

In the United Kingdom the deregulation programme has covered a number of service industries, most noticeably in the transport and financial services sectors, as well as public utilities including telephones, water, gas and electricity. For example, the government has tried to encourage new entry and make existing firms more efficient (e.g. through the introduction of more flexible work patterns) into both long-distance coach services and local buses services through the Transport Acts of 1980 and 1985, respectively.

Of all the markets to have been deregulated in the United Kingdom, however, perhaps the most drastic changes to have arisen have been in the financial sector where, following the Financial Services Act 1986, deregulation has brought about significant changes not only in the composition of the firms operating in each sub-market but also in the practices and manner of market conduct and the strategies employed by the firms.

Further legislation has been directed towards liberating particular markets, e.g. the Building Society Act 1987 has allowed building societies to offer unsecured loans, current accounts similar to banks and become estate agents and insurance agents, while the Social Security Act 1987 has meant that individuals are no longer tied to their company pension schemes (and can contract out of SERPS) and has led to a rapidly growing personal pension market. In support of these moves recent Finance Acts have also encouraged the development of new financial products such as TESSAs and PEPs for savings and mortgages.

The deregulation has opened up companies to increasing levels of competition, both nationally and globally. Previously the financial services industry could be divided into well-defined, separate sets of institutions with one particular core activity, such as banking, mortgage lending or insurance. There was no direct competition between strategic groups in their own particular segment of the 'industry'. Change began gradually with marginal regulatory changes. Increasing market saturation in core businesses led firms to attempt to expand their business scope. The barriers between strategic groups started to break down as firms diversified into broader financial portfolios. Firms are still defined by their core interests, banking, insurance or building society (although we have seen an example of the latter redefining itself as a bank in the case of Abbey National) but the idea of discrete, compartmentalized industry segments limited to specialized firms no longer applies. The financial services sector is intensely competitive and made up of firms offering a range of diversified products. Financial firms have examined their portfolio of business units using portfolio management techniques and have tried to broaden their activities as a hedge against risk. In some cases where this has taken them away from their core competence, such as Prudential Insurance's foray into the estate agency market, this has proved disastrous. Non-deposit-taking new entrants such as retail stores – Marks & Spencer springs to mind – diversifying into financial services represent powerful new competition. British American Tobacco (BAT) illustrates that you can successfully combine the management of both financial services (insurance) with the manufacture of goods (cigarettes), though its results over the past couple of years illustrate the problems currently affecting financial services. While its manufacturing side has remained highly profitable, BAT has had a major problem with Eagle Star in its expansion into the high-risk commercial mortgage guarantee and domestic mortgage indemnity markets. This has caused profits to fall, and the problem has been further exacerbated by the recent recession in the United Kingdom and decline in the sector as a whole.

The old-style bank is coming under pressure from new 'financial supermarkets' offering a fuller range of services. For example, the largest British investment banking house, Charterhouse J. Rothschild, owns a merchant bank, a venture capital arm, a portfolio investment company, a securities brokerage, an asset management company for the wealthy, a life insurance company, a mutual fund and various other trading companies! One is also seeing a growing representation of the highly diversified US firms in the United Kingdom, often through acquisition or joint ventures with the relatively small UK merchant bankers and traders. The industry is becoming increasingly global and demanding. Money never sleeps!

Removing regulation means lifting barriers to entry. New competition enters. It also means increased choice for consumers as all the major types of financial institutions converge on the same competitive arena. It becomes more useful to think of the market not in terms of the institutional providers but in terms of customer choice between a variety of services. Such a view is represented in the figure below for personal financial services.

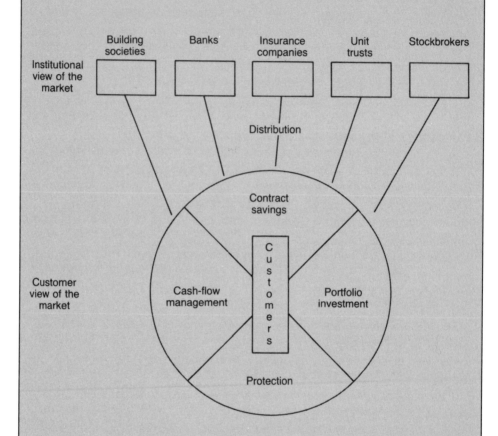

The switch from supply to demand orientation
*Source*: Ennew, Watkins and Wright (1990).

Competition across types of institution has recently focused on the following:

- mortgage provision (banks, building societies, insurance companies and specialist suppliers);
- the search for new young investors (banks and building societies – the market for higher education students has been highly

competitive with various offers to attract custom);
- money transmission services (banks and building societies);
- longer-term investment (insurance companies, unit trusts, stock brokers);
- higher interest accounts (banks and building societies).

Massive investment in new technology has moved service firms from a variable-cost, people-intensive industry to a fixed-cost base with high levels of employment breeding inefficiencies. One of the great management problems is how to use this new technology to increase white-collar productivity. Many financial service firms have gone through, and are still going through, painful restructuring – laying off employees to recoup their investment in technology, centralizing or contracting out low value added services such as basic data processing. Value chain analysis is applicable here to judge just what services need to be retained in-house and which can easily be contracted out more efficiently. Value chain analysis can also suggest to smaller firms where they might target their services to benefit from any contracting out that takes place. New technology has led to new business products. Increasing consumer power to access computer facilities is increasing the range of transactions. The new Smartcard credit card can combine financial transactions, credit/debit retailing, and personal, medical and other forms of information. In the new electronic banking environment technological innovation is a key factor in competition. The concept of the bank as a set of 'branches' is being replaced by increasingly sophisticated transaction machines.

The speed at which the changes have taken place in the financial services market can only in part be attributable to the technology that has recently become available. The fundamental cause of change and development in the markets has probably more to do with the inherent contestable nature of service markets where existing firms, unless protected by legal barriers to entry, may find it difficult to maintain high profit margins and exclude new firms if reputation and experience is easy to develop. Reputation and experience advantages, however, seem to be of diminishing importance and the financial giants may be squeezed as, in the short term at least, the markets become more competitive. Furthermore, there are a number of difficulties associated with running and organizing large financial conglomerates, e.g. witness the demise of British & Commonwealth in 1991.

Finally, even though we have emphasized, through Porter's (1980) structural analysis, that the firm's direction and performance (especially profitability) is likely to depend on the structure of the industry (where performance is likely to be stronger the fewer the competitors, the fewer substitutes available, the fewer the potential entrants, and the weaker the buyers and the suppliers), all of those factors may in fact actually work against the long-term position of the firm and the industry where lack of competition stifles the incentive to innovate and the firms cease to be dynamic and instead sit back and rest on their laurels.

Porter (1990) suggests that the lack of domestic competition and the weakness of related and supporting industries may have been a significant factor in accounting for the decline of many UK industries that once dominated world trade. In contrast, intense competition, e.g. in the Japanese consumer durable product industries (computers, electronics, cars, etc.) has spurred firms on to innovate new products, develop new processes and implement new management techniques to try to maintain their position and stay ahead of the competition. In terms of the 'competitive advantage of nations' the United Kingdom has lost all but a handful of its leading positions. While it still retains the dominant or at least a strong position in a number of service industries, including finance, insurance and auctioneering, most of the manufacturing side has declined, with the exception of pharmaceuticals, chemicals, cosmetics and some food and drink industries (e.g. whisky, confectionery and biscuits). The dominant position has been handed to other countries where domestic competition has been much stronger and consumers and other users have been far more demanding in terms of quality requirements.

The upshot of this is that no matter how good the business plan/strategy may be in principle, the firm may be hampered by the ineffectiveness of the supporting industries (i.e. the chief suppliers of equipment, inputs and business services) and the lack of suitably trained personnel. Thus ironically the long-term position of a firm may be enhanced by very tough competition, as a nasty tasting medicine, rather than the sweet situation of facing little or no competition.

**Review exercise**
Undertake a SWOT analysis of your company's position. What are the main opportunities facing the firm? Are current strategies appropriate to take advantage of these? Comment on the chief weaknesses of your organization. Suggest possible courses of action to remedy these.

# 3 Strategic choice

## Strategic considerations

The strategic options facing management are numerous. Management faces not only the problem of identifying options, but also evaluating each of them and then implementing the chosen ones. In selecting a strategy, the management should consider the choice with regard to (i) the competition facing the firm, and (ii) how the firm can develop (extend). These are the two most fundamental issues facing an organization. Large organizations, which have a diverse range of products, will also be interested in managing and developing their 'portfolio' of activities. This chapter examines each of these areas in turn:

1. competitive strategies;
2. development strategies;
3. portfolio strategies.

These strategies are concerned with the development of the organization in response to its internal and external environment. Based on the analysis of the firm's resources and capabilities, strategies should be designed to remove weaknesses and develop strengths, while pursuing opportunities and dealing with threats thrown up from environmental analysis. The implications for the firm may be a radical departure from current practices, such as reorganizing the firm's internal structure (e.g. breaking the organization down into separately functioning divisions) or entering new markets. On the other hand, new strategies may be a small progressive step from current ones, involving no internal upheaval with few adjustments in positioning the firm and little extension beyond current product range and targeted markets.

There are essentially three methods for developing the firm:

- internal development;
- mergers and acquisitions;
- joint ventures and agency dealings.

The choice between each method involves a trade-off between cost, speed and risk, while taking into consideration the strategies that rivals are following and how best to deal with the threat they pose. Both strategic direction and choice of method need to be considered in evaluating each option. In each case the option should be evaluated with reference to the following criteria:

- *Suitability* – 'strategic fit' in relation to the state of the internal and external environment (based on situation analysis).
- *Feasibility* – an assessment of how it might work in practice.
- *Acceptability* – consequences in terms of the risk and return to interested parties (i.e. shareholders, management, employees, etc.).

The firm's resources and the market conditions will have a large part to play in determining which options are most appropriate. If these conditions change, then so might the appropriate strategies. It is for this reason that the firm must continue to monitor its external and internal environment, regularly update its assessment of the options, and be ready to implement changes in strategies if necessary.

## Competitive strategies

The objective in selecting and following a well-defined 'competitive strategy' is to achieve *competitive advantage* – i.e. sustained superior profits compared to rivals. This comes from positioning a firm in the marketplace so that it has an edge in coping with competitive forces (outlined in the previous chapter) and in attracting buyers. The essential aspect to competitive advantage is that a viable number of buyers end up preferring the firm's product offering because of the 'superior value' they perceive it has. Superior value is created in two ways: either by offering buyers a 'standard' product at a lower price, or by using some differentiating technique to provide a 'better' product (i.e. higher perceived quality than rivals') that consumers are willing to pay a higher price for.

According to Michael Porter (1985), to achieve competitive advantage management is faced with a choice between one of three strategies, which he calls 'generic competitive strategies' (generic in the sense that they can be pursued in *any* market):

- *Cost-leadership strategy* – the firm strives to be the lowest-cost supplier and thus achieve superior profitability from an above-average price–cost margin.
- *(Product) differentiation strategy* – the firm strives to differentiate its product (or service) from rivals' products, such that it can raise price more than the cost of differentiating and thereby achieve superior profitability.
- *Focus strategy* – the firm concentrates on a particular segment of the market and applies either a cost-leadership or a differentiation strategy.

These options are represented in figure 3.1, where the firm has the choice between operating across the market – a broad-based strategy – or only operating in a limited part of the market – a focus strategy. In each case the firm should seek either a cost-leadership strategy or a differentiation strategy. Porter stresses that firms should not try to undertake more than one of these options.

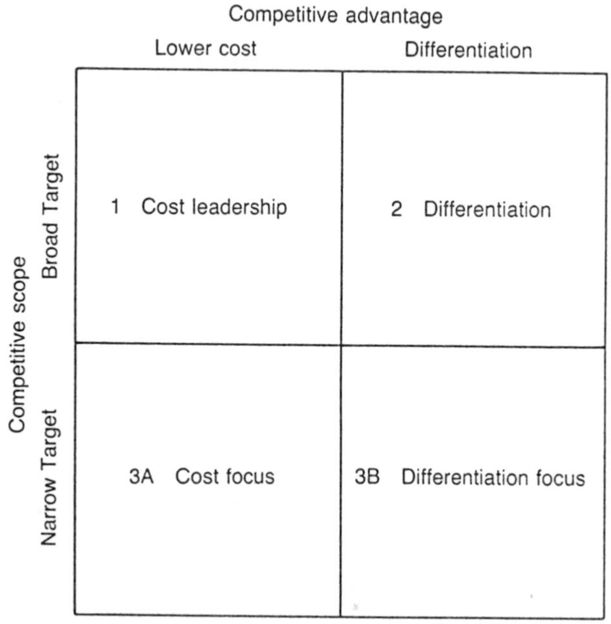

**Figure 3.1** Three generic strategies
*Source:* Porter (1985)

## Cost-leadership strategies

Examples of successful implementation of this strategy for the United Kingdom include BiC in ballpoint pens and disposable razors, Black & Decker in tools, Amstrad in consumer electronics, Aldi and KwikSave in the retail grocery trade, and the Superdrug chemist chain. In each case the firm has kept costs to a minimum and products basic.

The basic rules for following this strategy are that the firm should seek to 'cover the bases' (i.e. emulate the quality of other products available to the consumer at each quality-price level), 'trim the fat' (i.e. reduce costs by trimming the product down to its bare essentials required at each price-quality level), and use resources fully (e.g. fully utilize capacity). In addition, producing several brand names at once may allow the firm to gain a larger share of the market and subsequently reduce costs if economies of scale are available.

Striving for an overall low-cost position typically entails the firm being the leader in constructing the most efficient plants, implementing cost-reducing technological advances, keeping overhead and administrative costs to a minimum, and containing costs in R&D, advertising, service and distribution, while maintaining product quality. In particular, the firm should seek superior coordination across linkages in the value chain, while keeping costs to a minimum in each activity. Repositioning the firm may entail a fundamental internal shake-up, with working practices changed, automation extended, even relocation (closer to suppliers and/or customers).

The strategy is likely to be most successful when demand is price sensitive and the firms in the industry produce essentially standardized products, with competition being mainly in terms of prices. This could apply when buyers are not willing to pay the extra for differentiated products, or have common user requirements, or incur few switching costs in changing from one seller to another and are thus able to shop around for the best price.

There are attractive advantages in being the low-cost producer in an industry regarding defending oneself against the five competitive forces as defined by Porter (see chapter 2). In terms of industry rivalry, the low-cost company is in the best position to compete offensively on price. The low-cost company also has some protection over its profit margin when facing strong buyers since prices will rarely be bargained below the survival level of the next-most-efficient firm. The low-cost firm's greater efficiency also protects it from upward pressure on input prices; in addition, its high volume will give it increased bargaining power against suppliers.

Defending against potential entry is also made easier since its low-cost position will make it difficult for new firms to compete effectively on price, and the (credible) threat of a price war will also act as a barrier to entry. Furthermore, the low-cost firm is in a favourable position, compared to its rivals, to use price cuts to defend against competition from attractively priced substitutes.

There are, however, risks to following this strategy:

1.  Technological changes can result in cost or process breakthroughs which nullify past investments and efficiency gains. Staying on top of cost-saving technological improvements can be expensive, especially if it involves scrapping existing equipment.
2.  The advantage may be short-lived if rivals can easily imitate the leader's low-cost methods.
3.  There may be a shift in the market with consumers being less price sensitive and willing to pay for added quality and service features. Commitment to this particular strategy can often lead to strategic inflexibility, such that the firm cannot easily respond to changes.
4.  Strategic success in trying to be the low-cost producer requires the firm to be *the* overall cost leader, not just one of several firms vying for this position – for this would result in fierce competition and grim profit prospects until the leader was established and recognized.

By way of example of what can go wrong, exhibit 3.1 considers the strategy of the Ford Motor Company in the early part of this century. Ford developed mass manufacturing based on being the low-cost leader, an extremely successful strategy for over a decade, but failed to take into account the changing nature of the market with consumer preferences moving away from simply price to desiring more and different features. The problem arose because Ford's strategy of cost-leadership necessarily entailed inflexibility, notably in production, but this spread right across the value chain into other activities, so much so that when the market changed Ford could not respond. Since this episode Ford has remained a long way behind General Motors in terms of worldwide market share.

## Differentiation strategies

Successful differentiation strategies are not simply based on giving a product additional or different attributes to those of its rivals. Key elements in success are that buyers can see the differences, customers are willing to

---

### Exhibit 3.1   Cost-leadership backfiring

In the early 1900s Henry Ford froze the design of the famous Model T and concentrated on mass production at low cost. Motor chassis parts were completely interchangeable for the entire period 1909–26. The Model T's price was cut from $950 in 1909 to under $300 in the early 1920s. As a result Ford's market share increased from 9 per cent in 1909 to a high of 55 per cent in 1921. Thereafter, Ford failed to take into account the changing nature of consumer tastes and lost market share to General Motors.

While the Model T was economical and dependable, for about $100 more consumers could buy a Chevrolet, which offered not only a more pleasing style than the ungainly Ford, but also greater speed, better transmission, cooling, lubrication, ignition and springs. Consumers increasingly turned towards this car. Ford's market share fell to 41 per cent in 1925 and to 35 per cent in 1926.

*Sources*: Naylor, Vernon and Wertz (1983) and Lanzilloti (1961).

---

pay extra for the differentiated product, and rivals find it difficult to match the quality (attributes) of the product (either actual or as perceived by customers).

There a great many ways in which products and services can be differentiated, for example:

- Superior service – IBM in computers.
- Special features – The Apple Macintosh user-friendly personal computer.
- Overall value to the consumer – McDonald's.
- Product reliability – Johnson & Johnson in baby products.
- A complete line of products – General Motors automobiles.
- Top-of-the-line image and reputation – Rolls Royce cars.
- A different taste – Coca-Cola.
- Spare parts availability – Caterpillar, guaranteed delivery of parts within 48 hours.
- Engineering design and performance – Mercedes Benz cars.
- Unusual quality and distinctiveness – Rolex watches.
- Technological leadership – Sony in consumer electronics.
- Durability – Duracell batteries.

This list of approaches is not exhaustive. Successful differentiation strategies are numerous and can arise from any area or combination of areas in the value chain. For instance, the procurement of raw materials affects the performance and quality of the end product. Product-oriented R&D efforts lead to improved designs, performance features, product variety and being the first to come out with new models. Process-orientated R&D efforts lead to improved quality, reliability and product appearance. Emphasis on the manufacturing process can give consistent product quality, maintenance-free use and long-term durability. The emphasis on the outbound logistics system can lead to improved delivery time and accurate order-filling. Marketing, sales and customer service activities can result in quicker order processing, more and better training for end-users, faster maintenance and greater customer convenience.

As with successful cost-leadership, successful differentiation creates lines of defence for dealing with the five competitive forces. Firstly, it raises the firm above intense price competition rivalry within the industry. Secondly, it acts as a barrier to entry in the form of customer loyalty and uniqueness that new entrants must overcome. Thirdly, it puts the firm in a stronger position to ward off threats from substitutes due to its acquisition of a loyal clientele of customers. Fourthly, it reduces the bargaining power of buyers since the product alternatives are less attractive to them. Fifthly, it puts the firm in a stronger position with regard to bargaining with its suppliers, based on the high selling prices and given its position of eminence in the market. Successful differentiation acting as a defence against the competitive forces puts the firm in a position whereby it can secure high levels of profits.

The extent to which a firm is able to differentiate, given the nature of the market, depends on the skills and competencies available to it that competitors cannot easily match. Sustained competitive advantage is likely to come from four areas:

- technical superiority;
- quality;
- giving customers more support services;
- more value (for the same money).

Differentiation strategies are best suited to markets where there are many ways to differentiate the product or service and these differences are recognized by consumers to have value. This is especially so when buyers' needs and the uses of the item are diverse. Differentiation, as the word implies, means not following the crowd. In this sense it helps if few other firms are following a differentiation strategy.

Be warned – there are risks to following a differentiation strategy:

1.  The additional cost of adding enough product attributes to achieve differentiation can result in a selling price so high that buyers opt for lower-priced brands.
2.  Buyers may, over a period of time, decide that they do not need or want extra features, concluding that a basic model adequately serves their purposes, in which case emphasis is turned to low cost.
3.  Rivals may imitate the product attributes of the leaders to such an extent that buyers cannot sufficiently distinguish between the products. In this case the product developments of the firms cancel each other out and price becomes the main basis for competition.
4.  Continual product innovation is expensive but may be necessary to sustain competitive advantage. Breaking new ground only for followers to follow quickly and more cheaply may not be attractive.
5.  Broad-based differentiators may be out-manoeuvred by specialist firms focusing on one particular segment.

## Focus strategies

A focus or specialization strategy aims at building a competitive edge and carving out a market niche position by concentrating on only a portion of the market, e.g. concentrating on a particular group of consumers or a limited geographical market, or certain uses for the product. Examples of firms employing a focus strategy include Cray Computers (large mainframes), Rolls Royce (luxury cars), Land Rover (off-road vehicles), Ferrari (sports cars), Virgin Airways (low-cost transatlantic flight), Body Shop ('green' toiletries and cosmetics) and Norfrost (low-cost chest freezers).

Competitive advantage via focusing is won either by cost-leadership in the segment served or differentiation from meeting the needs of the target segment more effectively. This means either concentrating on cost-effectiveness for custom orders and short production runs, or providing unique and valued product features. The methods are very much the same as the broad-based cost-leadership and differentiation strategies outlined above.

Focusing is particularly attractive when there are distinctly different market segments, no other rival is attempting to specialize in the same segment, the firm's resources do not permit it to operate right across the market, and when segments differ widely in size, growth rate, profitability and intensity of the five competitive forces.

The successful focuser's specialized approach and unmatched skills in serving a limited market help it defend against the five competitive forces. Rivals do not have the same ability to serve the focused firm's clientele. Entry into the niche is made harder by the focuser's distinctive competence. This also acts as a hurdle that substitutes must overcome. The unwillingness of customers to shift their business to firms with lesser capabilities to serve their needs blunts their bargaining power.

As with the other generic strategies, there are risks involved in pursuing a focus strategy:

1. There is the possibility that broad-range competitors will find effective ways to match the focused firm in serving the target segment.
2. unfavourable shifts in buyer preferences may leave the focuser without a viable market, or in the case where buyers start demanding additional attributes, the segment may be taken over by a broad-based rival.
3. Competitors may find subsegments within the target segment and outfocus the focuser.

## Key features of the generic competitive strategies

### Overall low-cost leadership

- Production emphasis: 'nobody could do it cheaper'.
- Marketing/promotion emphasis: 'low, low prices' and 'outstanding value for money'.
- Operating culture: 'no frills' – reputation for being 'lean and mean'.
- Economies of scale from high volume: lower costs due to experience and bulk purchasing cost savings.
- Process innovations to cut costs.
- High productivity per employee.
- Price cutting as an offensive or defensive weapon.
- Low profit margins in return for high volume – 'stack 'em high and sell 'em cheap'.

### Broad differentiation

- Production emphasis: 'nobody could make it better'.
- Marketing/promotion emphasis: 'simply the best there is'.
- Operating culture: 'many frills' – 'the widest range of options/features' and 'something for every taste'.

- Create something different from competitors' products/services.
- Product innovation to bring new products with new options to the market.
- Premium pricing to cover added cost of differentiation.
- Intensive advertising and sales efforts.

*Focus*
- Production emphasis: 'we tailor our product to meet your particular needs'.
- Marketing/promotion emphasis: 'just for you'.
- Specialization – e.g. buyer segments, geographic areas, final-use applications: 'we're *not* a Jack-of-all-trades, we're a *master of one*'.
- Competitive advantage in the target segment depends on either (a) low-cost leadership (e.g. specialized experience/knowledge advantages); or (b) successful differentiation (e.g. offering something unique).

*Source:* Adapted from Thompson (1989).

This list provides a summary of the distinctive features of each of the generic competitive strategies. Which strategy is most appropriate will depend on the firm's current position and the nature of the products or services it provides. The current position is important because reorientating and consequently repositioning the firm may be no easy task and may involve substantial costs. For example, to pursue more rigorously a focused differentiation strategy may mean giving up existing customers if a move out of a market segment is required. Similarly, shifting emphasis towards low-cost leadership may mean giving up fairly successful differentiation advantages as the frills are dropped. But more importantly, repositioning the firm towards a particular competitive strategy is likely to be very expensive if it involves major internal adjustments (changing and reorganizing resources), and there may be a long time lag before the firm is able to operate both efficiently and effectively.

The nature of the product, in terms of how easily consumers can evaluate the quality, is likely to be a major influence on which the choice of strategy. 'Search' products, where consumers, and rivals, can easily evaluate the quality attributes of the product (prior to purchase), are typically best marketed by following a cost-leadership strategy, unless the firm's product has a unique (or far superior) search attribute that rivals cannot immediately emulate (e.g. Coca-Cola), in which case a differentiation strategy is appropriate (at least temporarily). On the other hand, 'experience' goods, where the product attributes are evaluated after purchase (e.g. food and modes of travel), offer more opportunities to pursue a successful differentiation strategy, since the attributes are less easily emulated by rivals. The same applies to 'credence' goods, where the attributes are only imperfectly evaluated even after purchases (e.g. competence of services provided by solicitors or accountants, and medical products) in which case the credibility of the seller, the brand name, and the firm's reputation become very important. In this latter case differentiation strategies emphasize 'perceived' quality, rather than actual quality.

Porter lays great emphasis on the firm only pursuing one of these competitive strategies, since otherwise it can fall into the trap of being 'stuck in the middle'. In this case it will be unable to compete effectively either in terms of price competition (won by the low-cost firm) or non-price competition (won by successful differentiators). A classic example might be British Leyland, especially in the 1970s. The message is that highest profits are to be achieved by specializing (in the strategic sense), otherwise profit prospects will be poor.

Nevertheless, it is not always easy to attribute a firm's success to how well it has undertaken a particular (generic) competitive strategy. An example is provided in exhibit 3.2 where Sainsbury's 'good food costs less' philosophy would seem to be a classic case of a firm falling between a cost-leadership position and being a leading differentiator. However, rather than being in the unenviable position of stuck in the middle and earning low profits with questions over its long-term survival, Sainsbury's is in fact the market leader in terms of market share and profit performance (its share of the retail grocery trade is 12.6 per cent and in 1990–1 it earned profits in excess of £500m). Furthermore, this is not the only example of a successful firm that, according to Porter's definition, ought to be stuck in the middle. A number of UK markets are dominated by such firms, e.g. Ford in cars, Cadbury's in chocolate, Bass in ales, Marks & Spencer in retail clothing, Prudential in insurance, Thomson in package holidays, Halifax Building Society in deposit account services and Barclays in current account services. One possible response to the accusation that they are stuck in the middle is that they are in fact successful differentiators offering 'best overall value' in their respective markets, and this has led to them becoming market leaders and has helped them maintain this position and become established household names.

## Exhibit 3.2  Is Sainsbury's 'stuck in the middle'?

Sainsbury's, the United Kingdom's largest supermarket chain, has the slogan 'good food costs less at Sainsbury's'. This essentially characterizes the market positioning of the company, targeting cost-conscious customers who place a high value on good-quality food. As the figure below illustrates, the slogan is an assertive expression of a position that is 'stuck in the middle'. This figure represents Sainsbury's taking the middle ground of the market. For example, its prices are above those of stores like KwikSave, but quality is not as highly as perceived as in stores like Marks & Spencer, where prices are higher.

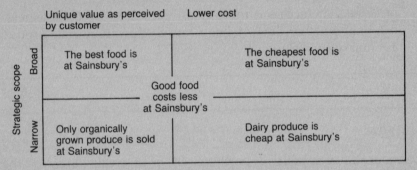

Sainsbury's have made strenuous efforts to keep costs down and at the same time maintain high quality. One of its primary corporate objectives is 'to provide unrivalled value to our customers in the quality of goods we sell, in the competitiveness of our prices and in the range of choices we offer'. To this end it has greatly extended its own-label products to up-market convenience foods, extended its fruit range to more exotic fare, and heavily invested in new technology, notably electronic scanning, to keep costs down and improve customer services.

The company has done remarkably well from its blending the twin goals of low cost and high quality. Its supermarket sales were well in excess of £6bn in 1990–1, and group pre-tax profits have grown at a rate of some 20 per cent p.a. over the last twelve years. Success, it would seem, has come about through neither focusing on consumers who were purely price conscious, nor pursuing quality regardless of price.

*Source*: Adapted from Cronshaw, Davis and Kay (1990).

**Questions**

1. Which competitive strategy would work best for your company? Would this involve a change from the present direction? If yes, do you think the costs of repositioning the firm would outweigh the benefits?

2. What, in your opinion, is the reason for Sainsbury's success? On British television, Porter claimed that Sainsbury's success is derived from its attempt to be a low-cost firm; it does not try to compete on quality with other firms. Is this plausible?

3. Do you think that the examples given of successful stuck-in-the-middle firms are likely to sustain their positions without concentrating on one particular competitive strategy? Is it possible that success is more to do with the way the business is run than whether the firm has a low-cost position or its products are markedly different from its rivals?

**Exercise**

Consider the competitive positions of your rivals. Identify their strengths in terms of (a) their cost position, (b) whether they have successfully differentiated their product(s) from the rest of the competition.

Are there any lessons to be learned?

Can you identify any unexplored but potentially profitable market niches?

## Directions for development

Devising a strategy for development involves making a decision, firstly, over which is the most appropriate direction for the company to move in, and secondly, on the most appropriate method. In this section we outline various strategic directions. The next section covers the methods.

The simplest way to depict the directions is in terms of the products made by the firm and the markets it operates in, as represented in figure 3.2

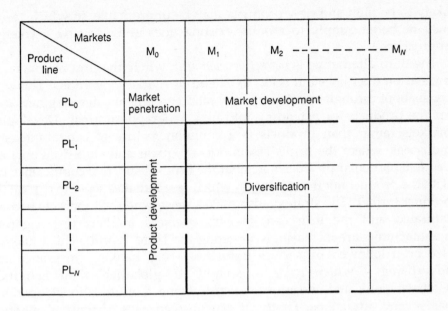

**Figure 3.2** Alternative directions for strategic development

– which should be familiar to you from the introductory chapter (figure 1.2). The diagram illustrates four directions.

Firstly, continue to operate in the same market with the same product. Growth in this situation, especially in a mature market, comes about through *market penetration*, whereby the firm increases its market share through improved quality or productivity or increasing its marketing activity. This is obviously an easier task if the market is growing. In static markets, the market leaders have advantageous cost structures (from economies of scale and the experience curve) over smaller firms, making market penetration more difficult. If market penetration is not feasible, then at least the firm may try for *consolidation*, where market share is maintained.

The second route is *product development*. Here the firm develops new products while maintaining the security of operating in its present markets. This direction is typically adopted in consumer-orientated industries where tastes are continually changing. For example, the short lifecycles of consumer electronics mean that product development needs to be a central part of company strategy. In retailing as well, we see firms continually introducing new product lines. This direction may be relatively easy to implement, particularly as it involves building on present knowledge and skills (especially in R&D). However, there are risks involved. Costs are likely to be high and new products may be unprofitable, in which case it may be better simply to modify existing lines and use new marketing approaches.

The third alternative is *market development*, where the firm maintains its present product lines but seeks to extend its market operations. This may come about through opening up new market segments, devising new uses for the products, or extending into new geographical areas. Developing markets rather than products is a common feature of capital-intensive industries, where the firm's assets (money, plant and skilled labour) are tied to a particular product, such that the firm's distinctive competence lies with the product not the market, in which case it makes sense to exploit the product further. The strategy also makes sense when old markets become saturated and the firm can develop overseas markets (e.g. cigarette manufacturers are increasingly targeting the Third World). This route has also been followed by service industries – e.g. banking, insurance and advertising – which have to sought to 'globalize' their activities. 'Globalization', and the move towards being a multinational operator, has several attractions. Firstly, it can be seen as a 'defensive' measure against tariff barriers and import controls. Secondly, it can be undertaken for logistical reasons over the costs of labour, transport and supplies. Thirdly, in capital-intensive industries globalization may have the benefit of switching away from declining home-based demand.

The fourth direction, and the most complex both in terms of implementation and options, is *diversification*, where the firm moves away from present products and present markets. We can distinguish two broad types: related diversification and unrelated diversification.

*Related diversification*
This involves increasing the range of activities in the value chain within which the organization undertakes itself, essentially through building and extending links in the chain. There are three different 'integration' directions. Firstly, the firm may choose to 'vertically integrate back-wards' towards its inputs, e.g. by producing its own raw materials or machinery, which may enable the firm to control better the quality, quantity and price of its inputs. Secondly, the firm can 'vertically integrate forwards' towards outputs, e.g. by moving into transport, distribution, retailing, or services and maintenance, to have more control over the final product market. Thirdly, it can 'integrate horizontally' towards substitute or complementary activities (e.g. by marketing by-products). In each case there may be productive efficiency gains, a better use of resources and a

wider spread of risk as the range of activities is increased; competitors may also be removed by blocking distribution or restricting supplies. There may, however, be disadvantages in the form of management over-extending itself into unusual areas where it has no expertise or experience (e.g. from manufacturing into retailing). Furthermore, by vertically integrating, the firm is more exposed to, and dependent on, the market, and its extended chain of activities makes it less flexible: if the market should dramatically change it may find it difficult to respond and reposition.

### Unrelated diversification

This covers options that lie beyond the boundaries of the industry within which the company presently operates. This route is most likely to be appropriate when the firm's current markets are saturated and/or declining, or when significant growth is sought but the firm's existing markets are small and offer few development opportunities. The kind of activities sought are usually complementary to current activities, either in terms of resources or finances. *Synergy* may be generated by the firm undertaking complementary activities where their combined effect, either in cost savings or profits, is greater than the 'sum of their parts' $(2 + 2 = 5!)$. For example, an underused refrigeration plant for meat storage could also be used for other frozen products, such as ice-cream. This type of cost saving, where the cost of joint production is lower than separate production, is often referred to as an 'economy of scope' and can arise when resources (labour, production capacity and plant) are underutilized. There may also be financial advantages to unrelated diversification. For example, a firm may undertake an activity designed to generate short-term positive cash flows because its main activity needs a source of cash. Also, the firm can spread its risks by not putting all its eggs in one basket. By having a portfolio of activities the firm can smooth out the effects of market and business cycles, even seasonal factors, to maintain constant cash/profit flows, which can be used to finance further growth. Nevertheless, of all the directions for development this route may prove to be the most tortuous. The firm may have to be internally restructured to form a 'divisionalized' firm. This may itself lead to a large management bureaucracy, with poor communication and control mechanisms, compounded by senior management moving into unfamiliar areas. It is often this route which leads to the downfall of many organizations because they simply overextend themselves (both financially and in terms of resources).

**Question**

Consider the direction your firm is likely to move to next. What pitfalls do you think await the firm? What actions do you propose to safeguard the firm?

## Methods for development

There are a number of methods for following a particular development direction. These methods fall into three categories:

- internal development;
- acquisition;
- joint development and agency relations.

The choice between them will to a large extent be dictated by the firm's resources and the market conditions, though preferences will be built up by management's own experience of each type. The choice reflects the degree of ownership and control that the organization requires. Internal development or acquisition allow for full ownership and control, where new activities are integrated into the organization. On the other hand, a move towards partial ownership and control would be reflected in a minority shareholding or a joint venture, whereas licensing, franchising and long-term contracting offer partial control without ownership.

### 1  Internal development

This method of development appears most appropriate when the activity requires a build-up of knowledge and skills – especially if they are highly technical in design or methods of manufacture. It may well be the only method for small companies to develop since they have no other choice due to lack of resources. In addition, it is also the only method open to the firm when it is developing new products or new markets, since it is breaking new ground.

Internal development necessarily involves a slower rate of change, which has the benefit of minimizing disruption within the organization. On the other hand its slowness may mean that opportunities are lost or not fully exploited.

## 2   Acquisition

Acquisition enables the firm to enter new product or market areas with greater speed than through internal development. The firm can acquire expertise, e.g. R&D, knowledge of markets and products, or a particular type of production system, all of which may have taken years to develop internally. Acquisitions also offer the firm the opportunity of a 'cheap buy'; if the target firm is going into liquidation, the acquirer can buy it cheaply and 'asset-strip' the firm (i.e. dispose of undervalued assets in a piecemeal fashion). This method also offers a quick and relatively painless way of entering static mature markets, since acquisition reduces the risk of competitor reaction. Cost efficiency may also be a key consideration if learning and experience curve effects are important in the industry, since the organization can overcome these problems by acquiring an experienced (cost-efficient) firm.

The major problem with acquisition (apart from paying too much!) is integration with other parts of the business. For example, business practices between the two organizations, such as the way activities are conducted, monitored and supported, may be fundamentally different and company cultures (and philosophies) incompatible.

## 3   Joint development

This method has become increasingly popular since the early 1970s and is currently extremely fashionable. This involves the firm entering into 'partnership' (via a contractual arrangement) with another party (a firm or even an individual) to undertake a business task. There are a variety of methods, each differing in their legal status, in terms of the balance of the partnership, and their purpose.

A 'joint venture' usually involves the setting up, by two or more companies, of a jointly owned, independent organization. The 'parent' companies share the costs and rewards (both profits and gained technologies/expertise). These arrangements offer flexibility, both strategically, since they generally do not tie up all the firm's resources, and because they can be dissolved relatively easily. The exception is with 'consortia', contractually obliged to finish a project, which are especially associated with large civil engineering projects (e.g. the Thames flood barrier). Joint ventures are generally undertaken for mutual interest. For instance, one side may gain technological expertise while the other gains access to different markets (e.g. the Rover–Honda link up, or joint ventures with East European firms such as the Volkswagen–Skoda deal), or because a project is so expensive that a number of companies decide to pool resources to share the risks (e.g. the European Airbus). As a defensive ploy joint ventures can be used to reduce competition, or act as a 'poison pill' to thwart a take-over attempt. Alternatively it can be used as an offensive strategy, where two firms link up to put pressure on a common competitor. Nevertheless, though there are many advantages to creating joint ventures, they tend not to last more than a few years, either because they complete their project (task), or because of difficulties encountered in running them. Difficulties can arise because of the influence exerted by the parent companies and the divided loyalties of management, which result in the joint venture losing its direction.

Another popular alternative is 'franchising', where the established firm sells the right to its product/brand name for another party to exploit, e.g. McDonald's, Body Shop, Kentucky Fried Chicken. This has advantages for both sides. The franchiser has the flexibility to change franchisees and can concentrate on its core business, while the franchisee can use an established brand name, backed up with mass consumer advertising and training, on a relatively small capital basis.

If the firm feels unable or is strategically unwilling to produce for all markets, it may have the option of 'licensing' its product or manufacturing process to another party. Licensing is more common in industries where patents and trade marks feature widely, e.g. in the pharmaceuticals industry or the brewing industry. In this case the firm offers a license to manufacturers, who pay a percentage of turnover to the firm. This route is useful for developing overseas markets.

Another alternative is to use 'agents' to conduct part (usually on the fringe) of the firm's business. For example, the company may prefer to use agents in small overseas markets. As well as being cost efficient compared to the alternative of maintaining permanent staff, the advantage of using local agents is that they have local knowledge of the market, culture and customs.

## Questions

1. What method has your company traditionally relied on for development? What have been the benefits and costs to the company?
2. What difficulties do you think would be encountered if your company acquired a vertically related business concern (e.g. a

retailer, or input supplier)? How long in your view would it take to overcome these problems?

3. Assuming that there is some scope for your business to undertake a joint venture, what purpose would be best served by such a venture. What would you realistically expect to gain from this joint venture? What would be the costs to the firm?

## Portfolio strategies

In this section we consider the management of the diversified firm's portfolio of activities/products, where strategy is developed to cover the overall interests of the company rather than simply the component parts. Thus strategy may well be aimed at maintaining a balanced portfolio of activities where certain parts are generating profits and significant positive cash-flow while other parts are growing towards this position. The firm is then viewed as a continuing process, whereas in contrast its products are seen as having only a limited lifespan.

The approaches we concentrate on are based on representing the portfolio in terms of its strengths and weakness. The first, and most influential, approach is the Boston Consulting Group (BCG) *growth–share matrix*. Other approaches are, in the main, extensions of this approach, such as the General Electric/McKinsey Industry attractiveness–strengths matrix.

The growth–share matrix was developed by the BCG as a means of enhancing diversified companies' portfolio performance by identifying which products to invest in, which to milk for funds, and which to eliminate from the portfolio. The BCG matrix, as depicted in figure 3.3, shows the position of the firm's products in terms of their market share and the growth rate of their market.

Market growth is measured, in real (i.e. inflation-adjusted) terms, as the growth rate per year of the overall market for the product. The rate is calculated either as an absolute figure or relative to that of real GNP. Market share of the product in its own industry can also be measured in two ways: either as a straight percentage or as that percentage deflated by that of the leading firm (as a measure of 'market dominance'). The emphasis on the largest competitor is based on the relative cost implications of BCG's theory of experience effects, which claims that the firm with the largest market share will often have the greatest accumulated experience and thereby the lowest unit costs. The growth emphasis is

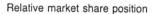

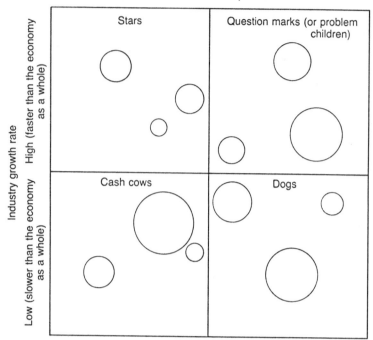

**Figure 3.3** The BCG growth–share business portfolio matrix

based on the product lifecycle model, where growth is taken to be a measure of industry attractiveness.

Products in each quadrant are assigned names based on their generation and use of cash, as well as their potential:

- *Stars* High growth and high share. These are strongly placed in the growth phase of the product lifecycle. Although cash generation is strong, it may not be sufficient to finance the rapid growth. As the market matures and slows, excess cash should be generated.
- *Question marks* (a.k.a. 'problem children') Low share of a growing market suggests that considerable cash is required to maintain share. Investment to create a star is risky.
- *Cash cows* Dominant products in a mature market produce excess cash that can be invested in stars and question marks.
- *Dogs* Low-share products in low-growth markets. Cash flow is usually low and can be negative due to a weak competitive position. If investment is required to maintain the share of a dog, it may be better to divest it and reallocate funds to a star or question mark.

The sizes of the circles in the diagram indicate the size of revenues generated. The boundaries separating the quadrants in the matrix are to some extent arbitrary. The market growth boundary is usually set at 10 per cent and the market share boundary at 1.0, i.e. parity with the market share of the largest competitor.

Viewed in terms of a product's development and lifecycle, we see heavy investment at the question-mark stage, hopefully turning this into a star, from which, as the market matures, it turns into a cash cow, which generates funds for investing in a new question mark or research and development, and so the process continues. The company should thus be careful to protect cash cows since these supply the funds for future growth. The marketing tools to adopt for question marks and dogs range from identifying new target segments and exploiting them, to cutting losses by divesting – either selling to another firm or via a 'management (a.k.a. leveraged) buy-out'.

While being useful in terms of the analysis it provides for directing investment across the portfolio, the approach does have some drawbacks. It is mainly concerned with describing the uses of cash flows and relies too heavily on the notions of product lifecycles and cost efficiency resulting from experience/market share. Furthermore, according to the matrix's boundaries most firms' products would fall into the dog category! Only a very limited number of products would seem, by definition, to reside outside this quadrant (there can only be one or possibly two products in the cash cow or star category). This begs the question why we see firms retain these 'dog' products. It would seem highly unlikely that firms keep dogs simply because they are unable to divest. A more plausible explanation is that they are in fact useful. Dogs do not cost much to feed and they may be useful in keeping predators at bay and stopping intruders. Indeed dogs may even be profitable. While the BCG approach relies on the argument of cost efficiency for generating profits, it neglects the point that a small market share can still result in high profits if product quality is high or unique. Furthermore, simply following the BCG's rules of taking cash away from cash cows and discarding dogs is likely to have very adverse effects on management and employee motivation in such areas of the corporation.

The BCG approach's limitations are in part due to its measures of business strength ('market share') and market attractiveness ('growth rates'). A number of other approaches have been proposed which seek to generalize the BCG matrix. The General Electric/McKinsey attractiveness–strengths matrix approach has a more broadly defined measures of industry attractiveness and the business's competitive standing. Figure 3.4

illustrates the GE matrix. There are several internal and external environmental factors that need to be considered before determining the position of each product. Business strength is measured in terms of the organization's ability and relative competitive position and so takes into consideration relative market share; profit margins relative to competitors; ability to compete on price and quality; knowledge of customer and market; competitive strengths and weaknesses; technological capability; employee relations and goodwill; and the calibre of the management. On the other hand, long-term industry attractiveness is measured with reference to the operating and general environment and addresses market size and its growth rate; industry profit margins (both historic and projected); competitive intensity; economies of scale; the nature of demand (e.g. cyclicality); technology and capital requirements; barriers to entry and exit; social, environmental and legal impacts; and emerging opportunities and threats. As with the BCG matrix, the sizes of the circles indicate the amount of revenues generated, while the shaded pie area in each circle represents the product's market share (the larger the black area, the larger

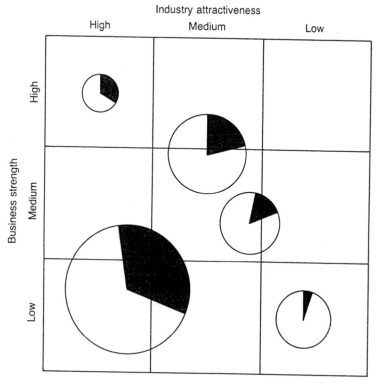

**Figure 3.4**   General Electric's nine-cell business portfolio matrix

share the product has of its particular market).

The GE matrix is certainly more complex, having nine cells compared to BCG's four. It is also harder to classify accurately each product into a cell due to the more ambiguous interpretation of 'strength' and 'attractiveness'. To determine each product's position, management needs to decide on the weight of importance they attach to each feature making up business strength and market attractiveness. This in itself it is not an easy task, and will certainly be very time consuming!

The general prescriptions for business policy are similar to those emanating from the BCG approach: maximize investment in strong businesses in highly attractive industries, undertake selective investment in activities which have market potential, specialize when business strengths are low but the industry is attractive, divest weak businesses in unattractive industries.

---

### Questions

In arguing against a firm necessarily choosing to divest a 'dog' division, John Seeger (1984) presents the following analogy:

> Divesting [such a] division would be analogous to a fire company's disposing of its Dalmatian hound. The dog does not contribute much to the direct function of putting out fires. But it looks good in photographs; it makes life more pleasant for the firefighters during their boring waits for alarms; and it keeps other dogs from pissing on the equipment.

1. What points is the analogy trying to make?
2. Under what circumstances would you keep a 'dog'?

---

## Dealing with the opposition

Strategic decisions are not, of course, taken in isolation from competitors' business plans. The organization must know who are its actual and potential competitors and assess their likely response to the organization's strategy. The strategist is then faced with the task of devising a plan of campaign to beat or at least neutralize these competitors to protect its market position.

In this subsection we consider some strategies, and the tools (or weapons!) that the firm can use, to beat the opposition in order to gain dominance in a market segment and then protect it. [See Ennew (1993) for a complementary account on developing and implementing marketing strategy.] A distinction should be made with regard to whether we are concerned with a new market or an existing market with several competitors. In the former case, if the firm is the sole operator, say through inventing a new product, and is the first firm in a newly created market, it is in a monopoly position. We are then concerned with how to protect this position and prevent new entry from other organizations.

Being the first firm into a market may give the firm a so-called 'first-mover advantage' over other firms. This advantage arises when the existing (i.e. incumbent) firm has natural advantages over other firms, say due to experience effects making its costs lower than rivals' and reputation and/or brand loyalty effects to make consumers unwilling to try another firm's product. These 'natural' barriers to entry can also be enhanced by 'strategic' barriers to entry, where the organization's deliberate actions seek to make entry difficult. Strategic actions may involve direct pre-emptive strategies, say by continued product innovation or by creating the industry standard (e.g. the IBM personal computer) and protecting it by patent to make further entry into the segment unprofitable. Alternatively, it may involve the organization taking a more aggressive action to convince a likely entrant that it is not in its best interests to enter the market by (credibly) threatening to use predatory behaviour. This may take the form of building extra plant capacity to fight a price war; or tying up all available raw material suppliers with long-term contracts; or tying up a distribution network to foreclose the market unless the entrant can enter as a vertically integrated firm making its own inputs and selling its own output to final consumers.

In established markets strategic actions are likely to be undertaken for a different purpose. While it is still important to prevent new entry, the organization is probably more likely to be concerned with existing rivals and the competitive pressures they pose. In established and especially mature markets, the organization may be faced with several competitors offering broadly similar products and operating with similar cost structures. This can lead to intense rivalry, and the firm may be concerned with developing and implementing policies aimed at changing its operating environment to make competition less fierce. Of course, differentiation strategies are directed towards this intense competition problem, but the firm also has the opportunity to alter the business environment by using either *aggressive* (a.k.a. *non-cooperative*) strategies to remove existing rivals from the scene. They may do this by forcing rivals out of the market through predatory behaviour, say by initiating and winning a price war and thus establishing a reputation for responding aggressively and so making other firms think carefully about moving onto their 'patch' in the market; or by using *cooperative* strategies to induce the other firms to behave more cooperatively and lessen the intensity of competition through collusion, e.g. by price information sharing schemes and forming strategic alliances.

A recent questionnaire survey of 377 UK companies involved in manufacturing and (financial) services conducted by Singh, Utton and Waterson (1991a,b) has shown how the use of strategic policies by companies to deal with competitors varies between established markets and markets for new products and also across different sectors of industry. Table 3.1 illustrates the ranking that firms assign to a variety of strategic tools in four sectors of the UK economy for both competition with existing products and dissuading entry of new products.

**Table 3.1**   Importance of strategic tools

| Policy | Chemicals/ pharmaceuticals | Electricals | Food/drink | Financial services |
|---|---|---|---|---|
| Patenting | 5/5 | 6/6 | 7/7 | 5/5 |
| R&D | 1/1 | 1/1 | 1/1 | 2/3 |
| Advertising | 6/6 | 5/5 | 4/5 | 4/4 |
| Capacity creation | 7/7 | 7/7 | 6/6 | NA |
| Pricing policy | 4/4 | 2/3 | 5/3 | 3/2 |
| Assured supply of materials | 2/3 | 4/4 | 3/3 | NA |
| Selling network for products | 3/2 | 3/2 | 2/2 | 1/1 |

*Note*: 1 is the highest ranking. The first figure is rank in existing firm competition, the second relates to new products.
*Source*: Singh, Utton and Waterson (1991a).

Table 3.1 reveals that the main tool used is R&D. The authors of the study found that this was primarily attributable to firms giving high priority to continuous improvement of the quality of the product launched (i.e. for product development) or to modifying products to sell overseas (i.e. for market extension). Other motives cited for using R&D included finding derivatives to plug gaps where competitors could enter (i.e. a strategy of 'brand proliferation', e.g. consider the product range of Procter & Gamble and Unilever in the household detergents market or Kelloggs in the ready-to-eat breakfast cereals market) and keeping pace with other firms' imitative products (especially in the electricals sector where technological opportunity is high). However, even though R&D was seen as the main competitive weapon, protecting these innovations by patents was seen as having a low priority. This suggests that the nature of R&D is for incremental innovation rather than for fundamental innovation. Only in the chemicals and pharmaceutical sector (where, incidently, the United Kingdom does have international market leaders) do patents assume some importance.

Advertising was, somewhat surprisingly, not ranked especially high. Its main purpose was to ensure sales for new products. Only in the food/drinks sector was advertising seen as being important over the product lifecycle to build and maintain brand loyalty. Similarly, pricing policy was not viewed as being especially useful, possibly because of the recognized dangers to profitability of price wars. The chief exception was in the electricals market for established products. Competition here to establish market share can be cut-throat: lifecycles are fairly short and heavy R&D and product launching costs must be recouped. In general, prices were determined by a standard cost plus mark-up procedure, with firms seemingly trying to 'meet' rather than 'beat' the competition.

Apart from R&D, the other chief policies appear to be concerned with the vertical linkage in the market, i.e. between suppliers and buyers. Both the use of long-term buying contracts with suppliers (giving assured supply for the firm while at the same time limiting availability of raw materials to new entrants) and by creating distribution networks through which the organization's products can be sold (preferably on an exclusive dealing basis) appear to be widely used in the manufacturing sector. Both of these tactics are important for long-run performance beyond the lifecycle of the current product range. They make entry into the market difficult for new players, but make it relatively easy for the organization to successfully bring new products to the market by having the input suppliers lined up and 'guaranteed' outlets for the new products.

According to the survey, countering the competitor's move was viewed as the best way to react to entry. In the manufacturing sector this generally means altering the product range, by updating or providing additional features, or looking for new markets in which to sell the existing product. Copying the competitor's product was not a common reaction, nor was the use of price-cutting or intensive advertising and other promotional activity.

A slightly different picture emerges in a similar type of questionnaire study by Smiley (1988) on strategies that US firms use to deter entry. Contrary to the above findings for the United Kingdom, Smiley's study found that advertising to build up brand loyalty was the most widely used and best-regarded weapon to prevent entry and protect market share in markets for both new and existing products. R&D (including patenting) was found to be the second most used tactic, but seen as significantly less important than advertising in markets for established products. As in the UK study, attempting to foreclose markets through distribution channels or input purchases was also widely used, while price policy (e.g. keeping prices low to make the market appear unattractive to potential entrants) and excessive capacity creation (to show how aggressively the firm would respond to entry) were rarely used.

## Selecting appropriate strategies

Now that you have some idea of the range of options facing you, there remains the 'slight' problem of choosing between them! In our view there are three key criteria on which to make a basis for a decision:

- suitability;
- feasibility;
- acceptability.

We briefly outline the issues surrounding each aspect in turn.

### Suitability

To be 'suitable' the strategy should fit the needs of the firm in terms of exploiting strengths and grasping opportunities while defending against weaknesses and threats. The appropriateness of a strategy will be judged on the basis of how well it tackles the issues in the external environment and how effectively it can use and develop the firm's resources. The strategist must then relate back plausible options to situation analysis, say via the SWOT procedure outlined in the previous chapter, to see how well the strategy deals with the internal and external environmental conditions. While simple techniques like SWOT are useful, a fuller analysis will be required, taking into consideration how well objectives are likely to be met, e.g. competitive advantage, synergy, lifecycle development and product portfolio development. It is also important for a firm embarking on acquisition and/or joint ventures that it considers cultural fit between the organizations.

## Feasibility

This concerns whether or not a strategy can be implemented successfully. To implement a strategy the firm must have or be able to obtain the necessary funds, along with the necessary materials, services, technology and managerial, marketing and operative skills. Management must also be sure that the organization is capable of performing to the required level (overall and in the specific areas of the value chain). It should also take into consideration whether the desired or target market position can be achieved.

In terms of resource planning the firm should use various finance techniques to assess feasibility, e.g. study the implications for funds (cash) flow and consider the 'breakeven' situation and how attainable this is (Davidson and Mallin, 1993).

## Acceptability

There seems little point in undertaking a strategy if the end result is likely to be unacceptable to senior management, shareholders and other interested parties (e.g. employees, government, customers and suppliers). Strategies should therefore be assessed in terms of likely returns, e.g. profitability and growth rates, the risks attached to each strategy (especially financial risks, e.g. to liquidity), their effects on the firm's environment, and whether it 'fits existing systems' within the organization (i.e. keeping internal changes to the necessary minimum, keeping activities in balance).

Management should be quite clear on expected profitability rates, especially anticipated 'return on capital employed' (ROCE) and pay-back rates (i.e. time taken to pay back the invested capital by estimating net cash flows or discounted cash flows). The effect of the strategy on the firm's 'capital structure' (i.e. balance of debt and equity) will be a key measure of financial risk. Scenarios should also be used to examine worst, best and most-likely outcomes.

It goes without saying that the best route to follow is the one that is most suitable, feasible and acceptable. Unfortunately life is not so easy and management will be faced with choosing between strategies that are not unambiguously ranked. In this case they will have to decide on which strategy offers the best overall compromise to best meet their objectives.

## Conclusion

The criteria used to determine the appropriate strategy and the means or tools for implementing it are as likely to depend on the make-up of the organization (and the preferences of key individuals) as the industry and culture in which it operates. Certainly, it appears that there are national differences in the key goals of business leaders which suggest that in different countries particular strategies might be more common than in other countries. Similarly, industry norms may dictate the kind of strategies that are followed, or at least limit the number of viable options.

By way of illustration of national differences, table 3.2 summarizes the findings of a comparative survey of top managers in 1,031 Japanese and 1,000 US industrial corporations in the early 1980s. The managers were asked how important eight diverse goals were to their organizations. The table shows the average rankings for the two panels. In the United States the managers seem to go for traditional profit-maximizing targets – return on investment and higher stock prices. In Japan, however, companies appear to go for future earning potential – in particular forsaking short-term profits in favour of introducing new products that enhance long-run profit performance. This could be attributable to a number of factors. For

**Table 3.2** Ranking of business goals: a comparison between US and Japanese managers

| Goal | American managers | Japanese managers |
|---|---|---|
| Return on investment | 1 | 3 |
| Higher stock prices | 2 | 8 |
| Increased market share | 3 | 2 |
| Improving products and introducing new products | 4 | 1 |
| Streamlining production and distribution systems | 5 | 4 |
| High net worth ratio | 6 | 5 |
| Improvement of social image | 7 | 6 |
| Improving working conditions | 8 | 7 |

*Source*: Scherer and Ross (1989).

**Table 3.3**   Business objectives in the United Kingdom

| Primary objective | Percentage of respondents |
|---|---|
| To earn as large a return on capital as possible | 37% |
| To earn as large a return on sales as possible | 22% |
| To maintain the firm's market share | 15% |
| To maintain the firm's ranking in the market | 5% |
| To make as great an absolute amount of profit as possible | 22% |

*Source*: Adapted from Singh, Utton and Waterson (1991a).

instance, in the United States (as well as in the United Kingdom) the stock market acts as a market for 'corporate control', where takeovers displace senior management teams: the incentive is to keep share price high to maintain one's job! In Japan the stock market is not so effective at disciplining management teams in this way and the more important characteristic is the link between banks and companies, which allows the latter to go for long-term investment. This link is further supported by managers' long length of service – Japanese managers often have contracts for lifetime tenure. Alternatively, cultural differences may also explain the ranking of the goals. US managers have been concerned with short-term cost reduction; the Japanese have concentrated on the long-term development of technological competitiveness. Japanese businesses have strived since World War II to become internationally dominant in high-technology and high-value-added industries where the scope for product and process innovation (including the reorganization of methods of operation) is high (see Best, 1990).

As for the United Kingdom, business objectives seem to be broadly in line with the US picture. The recent survey by Singh, Utton and Waterson (1991a,b) of senior managers across 293 firms in manufacturing and financial services, as illustrated in table 3.3, again shows the primary objective to be based on a measure of immediate profit maximization – either return on capital or sales or absolute profits. The firm's position in the market is not generally seen as the chief business objective.

This survey of UK managers also revealed that the most common policies employed to achieve the primary objective were either through the introduction of new products or competitive actions taken against rivals. This illustrates the concern with keeping ahead of the market and viewing competitors' positions as being the main limitation on profit potential. As

**Table 3.4**  Policies to achieve main objective

| Policies | Percentage of respondents |
|---|---|
| Development of existing products | 3% |
| Development of existing production processes | 8% |
| Introduction of new or improved products in the same area | 53% |
| Competitive actions taken against rivals' new products (or new rivals) | 36% |

*Source*: Adapted from Singh, Utton and Waterson (1991a).

table 3.4 shows, developing existing products or processes is used far more rarely compared to the more aggressive policies concerned with innovation and attacking competitors' positions.

Of course, these more aggressive policies not only have the benefit of keeping the organization one step ahead of the competition (by fair means or foul!) but also alter the business environment to the advantage of the firm by creating new demand (or even a new market with a fundamentally new product) or by changing the structure of the industry to a more comfortable situation, say by inducing existing rivals to exit the market (e.g. through predatory pricing) or by preventing (viable) new entry. Indeed it is this mechanism to manipulate the industry environment that offers the organization the means for long-run superior performance over other firms.

---

### Review exercise

1. Following on from your SWOT analysis from the review exercise in chapter 2, identify the competitive strategy that most suits your company's needs. State your reasons for this choice.
2. State which direction you think the company should move towards along with a choice of method. Explain your reasons for this combination in terms of how feasible this option is. Is this the best option in terms of a balance between risk and return? If not, which option offers the most acceptable rewards?
3. What particular actions do see the firm pursuing to obtain and maintain a position of dominance in its markets?

4.  Who do you see as being the most serious threat to the market position of your organization? Do you consider the most likely threat to be a firm already competing in the market, a firm in a related industry, a supplier or buyer, or a foreign firm, or a new arrival (possibly from an entirely unrelated industry)?
5.  How would you deal with encroachment of your market position by an existing rival or new entrant?

# 4 Organization and strategy

## Organizational issues and strategy

In chapters 1–3 we have been concerned with what strategy is, how firms define their strategic goals and the nature of the business environment. In this chapter we look at the organizational factors that impact on strategic management. First of all we address the issue of how we should think about the nature of *organization* – what are the important factors that make up an organization and what it means to be well organized. We then turn to the question of organization *culture* – the values that hold organizations together. To clarify the relationship between organization, culture and strategy we look at the work of Peters and Waterman on Japanese management and strategic human resource management. Finally, we look at the issue of organization *design* and *structure* – how organizations are designed and run to enhance strategic responsiveness.

The key point we want to communicate is that the notion of organization subsumes a variety of variables, all of which impact on strategy. Traditionally, organization structure has been the factor most emphasized in the strategic management literature. The argument was that you decided upon your strategy and then designed an organization structure to support that strategy. Strategy, in this traditional view, determined structure. We now know that this is not always the case. Existing structures have important implications for strategy. They can facilitate strategy or impede it. And there are a range of other factors beside strategy that are important in strategic management.

Two key events were important in bringing the importance of organizational issues to the fore in considerations of strategic management. These were:

1. Peters and Waterman's best-selling book *In Search of Excellence*.
2. The success of Japanese firms in the West.

## Peters and Waterman's excellent organizations

According to Peters and Waterman, excellence in organizations is equated with the ability to change. Excellent organizations are continuously innovative, geared to quick action and regular experimentation:

> innovative companies are especially adroit at continually responding to change of any sort in their environments. . . . As the needs of their customers shift, the skills of their competitors improve, the mood of the public perturbates, the forces of international trade realign, and government regulations shift, these companies tack, revamp, adjust, transform, and adapt. In short, as a whole culture, they innovate.   (Peters and Waterman, 1982: 12)

Excellent companies are characterized by 'quick action, service to customers, practical innovation'. These are not possible without the commitment of the staff to company philosophy. Structures and systems that inhibit quick communication and action are anathema. The customer is the key element in the organization's environment. There are three 'pillars' necessary for excellence:

- the *stability* pillar – a simple, basic underlying form that generally corresponds to the old divisional product-based structure;
- the *entrepreneurial* pillar – entrepreneurial 'small is beautiful' units, which are problem-solving, and implementation groups and measurement systems based on the amount of entrepreneurship and implementation; and
- the *'habit-breaking'* pillar – a willingness and an ability to reorganize regularly on a temporary basis to create experimental project teams to attack specific problems. Regular reorganizing is a way to meet shifting pressures without putting in place huge, permanent integrating committee devices.

The three pillars represent a response to three prime needs: a need for efficiency around the basics; a need for regular innovation; and a need to avoid 'calcification' by ensuring responsiveness to major threats.

Hickman and Silva (1984), in an extension of Peters and Waterman's work, argue the need for managers to combine strategy and culture in seeking change by analysing customers and employers:

> While strategic thinking aims at getting and keeping customers, culture building attracts, develops, motivates, and unifies the right kind of employees . . . no matter how strongly an organization's culture motivates and develops

employees, if customers do not perceive better products and services as a result, the culture has been wasted. The intertwined relationship between customers and employees requires watchful management, by well-trained executives. (Hickman and Silva, 1984: 85–6)

Excellent organizations need to build and sustain excellent cultures by selecting, motivating, rewarding, retaining and unifying good employees. The goal is an organization of many hands but of one mind devoted to building the best product possible, fully satisfying customers and taking care of one's own people.

Key data for assessing an organization's culture are:

- *the organization's history* – the events, people and decisions that have shaped this history; how the organization has and is performing;
- *the dreams, ambitions and values of key personnel* – these key personnel are the 'opinion leaders', who can be both managers and employees;
- *organizational stories* (often called organizational myths) that contain key information relating to beliefs, values, concerns, rules (the do's and don'ts) and general ways of getting things done. There is a strong 'people' emphasis in excellent organizations – successful relationships grow from kindness, empathy and commitment. Motivation is important because people want to be stretched and relish challenges to their competence.

A key argument of Peters and Waterman is that there is more to organization than just structure. They demonstrate that the skilful management of seven factors is important for excellence. This argument leads to their 'seven Ss' framework depicted in figure 4.1.

They define their seven Ss as follows:

- *Strategy* – those actions that a company plans in response to or in anticipation of changes in its competitive environment and the way a company aims to sustain or improve its competitive position.
- *Structure* – the organization chart and related information that show how the work of the organization is divided up and then coordinated.
- *Systems* – all the procedures and processes that enable the organization to run from day by day, year by year, such as capital budgeting systems, employee relation systems, information systems.
- *Style* – tangible evidence of what management considers important as demonstrated by how it spends its time and how it uses symbolic behaviour. Peters and Waterman point out that it is not what

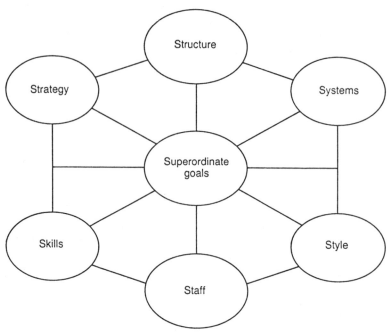

**Figure 4.1** The seven Ss framework
*Source*: Peters and Waterman (1982)

management say that is important, but the way it behaves. There can, in short, be a discrepancy between stated attitudes and actual behaviours. For example, most managers will say they are democratic. People reporting to them judge them as far more autocratic than they themselves think
- *Staff* – the people in the organization. Peters and Waterman argue that we should think about 'corporate demographics' both in its hard, quantitative sense – appraisal systems, pay scales, formal training, etc. – and in the soft, qualitative sense of morale, attitudes, motivation and behaviours.
- *Superordinate goals* – the shared values and guiding concepts that underpin the formal statement of corporate objectives. Compelling superordinate goals pull an organization together and provide stability over the long term. Peters and Waterman suggest that, unlike the other six Ss, superordinate goals do not seem to be present in most organizations but that they are a major feature of the excellent companies they studied. It is one of the main functions of leadership

to articulate these goals and, thereby, create a sense of meaning for employees.

- *Skills* – the capabilities possessed by the organization. These are more than just the sum of individual skills and require skilful management. Some organizations with highly skilled individuals do not possess the capability of actually harnessing these skills to get things done, while other organizations are able to perform extraordinary feats with apparently ordinary people.

The seven Ss framework illustrates two important facts. Firstly, the seven Ss cannot be treated in isolation from one another. The notion that if you get the structure right the people will automatically fit is simply wrong, as is the notion that if you get the right people then success is guaranteed. Structure and staff are important but so are the other five factors. Secondly, we need to take the 'soft' variables – style, systems, skills and superordinate goals – very seriously. They are at least as important as strategy and structure in achieving excellence. Take the problem of strategic change. It is very easy to state different strategic objectives, such as new target customers or new levels of product or service quality. It is relatively easy and quick to reorganize in the sense of changing one's structure, altering reporting relationships and so on. Hence the old managerial adage 'If you don't know what to do, reorganize.' But carrying these changes through is a far more difficult and lengthy process. A major change in systems to support a new strategy, a major retraining program to change the skills base of an organization or the generation of commitment throughout the organization to a new superordinate goal can take years. Peters and Waterman's final important point is that you need to think of the seven Ss as seven compass points. It is only when they are all aligned and pointing in the same direction that you can truly call yourself well organized.

---

### Question

How would you assess your organization's culture? Use the factors mentioned above – history, myths, etc. – to do this. What do these factors tell you about your organization's key values and beliefs?

## Japanese organizations and strategic management

> Culture arrived on the management scene in the 1980s like a typhoon blowing in from the far East.   (Quinn, Mintzberg and James, 1988: 344)

More specifically, the importance attributed to culture was due to the success of Japanese firms in markets such as consumer electronics and automobiles that had been traditionally dominated by Western firms. Culture is also a key issue in Peters and Waterman's work discussed in the last section. Excellent organizations are 'rich in culture', i.e. they are characterized by strong, shared systems of beliefs about where they are going and what kind of organization they are. Culture constitutes a deeply entrenched perspective which conditions the ways in which an organization sees the world, develops new ideas and responds to changes in the environment.

---

### Exhibit 4.1   Changing the culture of ICI

One of the hardest parts of Sir John Harvey-Jones's task in turning ICI around in the 1980s was to change the culture of the organization. The choice of a new strategic direction for the company was relatively easy, i.e the decision to de-emphasize its European business, to diversify into other geographic areas, particularly the United States, and to change the balance of its portfolio of products in favour of higher value-added chemicals with greater margins than the bulk commodity chemical business. There was also a series of acquisitions, over 100 in the 1980s. The difficult problem was to implement the new strategy, to make it happen. This necessitated culture change. To change the culture meant getting rid of people and teaching those that remained to think in a different way. A key aspect of the latter was to convince people to stop thinking as scientists and technologists ('This is an interesting product or technology') and to start thinking as business people ('This is a more profitable line of business'). This constituted a major new skills emphasis and a major task of rethinking the nature of the company and its values.

Culture has a crucial role to play in strategic management. An existing management culture helps determine ways of thinking about strategy, as exhibit 4.1 demonstrates. A change in strategic direction will often necessitate a change in culture. Perhaps its most crucial role is in determining the way in which people are selected, trained, developed and rewarded. Organizational culture determines the kind of people who will be attracted to a firm and the way they will interact within the firm. Peters and Waterman's ideal image is of a shared culture based on a feeling of collective interest and a shared system of beliefs, habits and traditions. Of course, this is not always the case. Indeed, some would say that such an organization is the exception rather than the norm and that organizations are fundamentally political entities built on self-interest not common interest, in which individuals and factions are, like Machiavellian princes, looking to build their own power bases at the expense of the common good.

The major examples of strong, shared, common cultures have been drawn from Japan. Akio Morita, the chairman of Sony, compares Japanese firms (*kaisha*) to families.

> There is no secret or hidden formula responsible for the success of the best Japanese companies. No theory or plan or government policy will make a business a success; that can only be done by people. The most important mission for a Japanese manager is to develop a healthy relationship with his employees, to create a family-like feeling within the corporation, a feeling that employees and managers share the same fate. Those companies that are most successful in Japan are those that have managed to create a shared sense of fate among all employees, what Americans call labor and management, and the shareholders. (Morita, 1987: 130)

Morita's words are echoed by Konosuke Matsushita, the founder of Matsushita Electrical Industrial Company, who compares Japan with the West in chilling tones.

> We will win and you will lose. You cannot do anything about it because your failure is an internal disease. Your companies are based on Taylor's principles. Worse, your heads are Taylorized too. You firmly believe that sound management means executives on the one side and workers on the other, on the one side men who think and on the other side men who can only work. For you, management is the art of smoothly transferring the executives's ideas to the workers' hands. We have passed the Taylor stage. We are aware that business has become terribly complex. Survival is very uncertain in an environment filled with risk, the unexpected, and competition. . . . We know

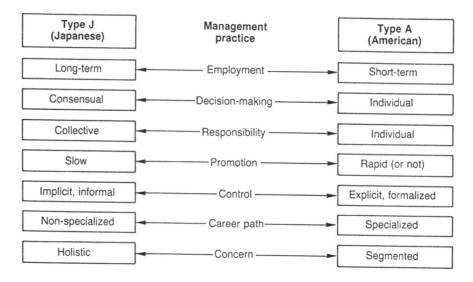

**Figure 4.2**  Type J versus type A organizations
*Source*: Adapted from Ouchi (1981)

that the intelligence of a few technocrats – even very bright ones – has become totally inadequate to face these challenges. Only the intellects of all employees can permit a company to live with the ups and downs and the requirements of the new environment. Yes, we will win and you will lose. For you are not able to rid your minds of the obsolete Taylorisms that we never had.   (Best, 1990: 1)

---

**Exhibit 4.2   Japanese and Western attitudes – I**

During a visit to a Japanese bank, both the Japanese president and the American vice-presidents of the bank accused the other of being unable to formulate objectives. The Americans meant that the Japanese president could not or would not give them explicit, quantified targets to attain over the next three or six months, while the Japanese meant that the Americans could not see that once they understood the company's philosophy, they would be able to deduce for themselves the proper objective for any conceivable situation.

*Source*: Ouchi (1981: 33–4).

William Ouchi, a noted American management scholar, has studied the contrast in management practise between Japanese and American firms. Figure 4.2 sets out his findings in terms of the differences he observed. The Japanese (type J) firm looks to create, through its management practices, a sense of 'holistic' concern. That is, it looks to generate in each individual a sense of commitment to the good of the whole organization.

---

**Question**

Would you describe British firms in general as more like type A or type J?

---

## Strategic human resource management

Studies of Japanese success have suggested a variety of reasons for their competitive advantage over the West. These reasons are summarized in figure 4.3.

Some claim it is government fiscal and monetary policy that has given Japan its edge. Similarly the role of the Japanese government in targeting research and development in particular industries as part of its industrial policy has been mentioned. Others suggest it is due to technology, that Japan has had access to advanced manufacturing systems, while Western firms make do with outdated machinery. Others argue that the differences are due to Japanese national culture, which very strongly values an ethic of hard work, commitment to the organization you work for and an education system that delivers highly skilled and motivated school-leavers and graduates. But it is the fourth factor, 'corporate management' and the Japanese approach to human resource management, that has been given most attention in the West as the source of their success. Japanese advantage, the argument goes, rests not on new technology or education or government policy, though these all play a minor role. It primarily depends on management's capacity to produce a near fault-free product cheaply through the diligent and skilful control of the system of production and the human factor.

What, then, is the link between the Japanese system of human resource management and strategic management? Let us look at Japanese

| | Macro | Micro |
|---|---|---|
| **Hardware** | **Government fiscal and monetary policies**<br><br>Taxation<br>Capital markets<br>Savings | **Production capability**<br><br>Plant<br>Equipment |
| **Software** | **Socio-economic environment**<br><br>Work ethic<br>Regulation<br>Education | **Corporate management**<br><br>Organization<br>Administration<br>Production system |

**Figure 4.3**   Key elements in manufacturing competitiveness
*Source*: Adapted from Abernathy, Clark and Cantrow (1981)

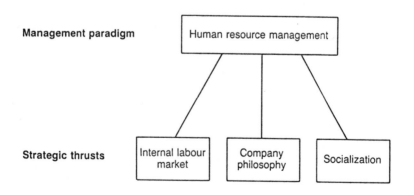

**Figure 4.4**   The Japanese management system
*Source*: Adapted from Pucik and Hatvany (1983)

management practices in more detail. The elements of the Japanese system are set out in figure 4.4.

A paradigm is a shared set of rules and intuitions about the way things can and should be done. The Japanese system has as its core a set of shared rules and beliefs about how to deal with human resources. This focus on human resources reflects the belief that a key source of strategic success is the maximum utilization of available human assets. It has three main strategic thrusts. First, the emphasis is on creating an internal labour market made up of employees with the desired skills, both technical and social. The goal of the management of the internal labour market is to induce employees to stay with the firm over the long-term, hence an emphasis on lifetime employment. Second comes the unique company philosophy to give employees a sense of meaning from their employment and a sense of where the organization is going in the future and what their role is in that future. Third, new employees undergo an intensive period of induction into the company to test that they possess the required characteristics and to teach them what it means to be part of the company.

---

### Exhibit 4.3   The Japanese ethic

In Japan, workers who spend a lot of time together develop an atmosphere of self-motivation, and it is the young employees who give the real impetus to this. Management officers, knowing that the company's ordinary business is being done by energetic and enthusiastic younger employees, can devote their time and effort to planning the future of the company. With this in mind, we think it unwise and unnecessary to define individual responsibility too clearly, because everyone is taught to act like a family member ready to do what is necessary.

*Source*: Morita (1987: 149).

---

The general strategic thrusts of the Japanese management system are operationalized through specific management techniques. Open communication is encouraged and supported. Employees' skills are developed continuously through job rotation, which focuses on a broad range of skills and ongoing training throughout their career. Employees are appraised on a variety of criteria, including contribution to team achievement, rather than just in terms of individual results. Work is structured so that it can be carried out by teams which are given the maximum autonomy possible. In return for this autonomy, teams are expected to exercise responsibility in the pursuit of agreed organizational goals. Decision-making is preceded by extensive consultation. Again, the return for being involved in the decision-making process is the expectation that individuals and groups will assume responsibility for implementing the decision. Concern between management and managed is seen as mutual. Employees are expected to become involved and managers are expected to foster employee participation in pursuit of the welfare of all.

This management style has a strong effect on business strategy. Long-term socialization linked to the commitment to a unique company philosophy fosters a competitive spirit in employees. The mission of the organization is to survive as a group by defeating the competition. Japanese industry in those sectors where they are world leaders is characterized by very intense levels of competition and Japanese managers are developed in an atmosphere of fierce competitive rivalry. This emphasis on competitiveness is reflected in the concern of Japanese firms with market share as a key business goal. This concern also reflects, in part, the goal of retaining core staff during periods of downturn when Japanese firms tend to cut prices to maintain market share rather than protect their margins by reducing output and employment. The management approach is based on a long-term perspective because employment is for the long-term and the firm exists to maximize all its members' interests. The emphasis is strongly on internal growth as a means of ensuring the survival of the corporation. Divestitures, mergers and acquisitions are unusual in Japan and strategy is based on continuous product and process innovation and improving quality while reducing costs.

The implications of the Japanese management system for business strategy can thus be summarized as follows:

1.  the generation of competitive spirit;
2.  an emphasis on market share;
3.  a long-term perspective;
4.  an emphasis on internal growth;
5.  the continuous search for innovation, quality improvement and cost reduction.

One final point. It has recently been claimed that there is one major feature of the Japanese approach to strategy that distinguishes it from that of most Western firms. This is *strategic intent* (Hamel and Prahalad, 1989). The

**Exhibit 4.4   Japanese and Western attitudes – II**

On the latter point, one of the authors was doing some work with a Japanese company. When he asked a Japanese manager what he saw as the key distinguishing factor between Japanese and Western employees, the Japanese manager answered that the biggest difference he had noticed came when a task had been completed. If they had done it well, the Western employees expected to be praised and rewarded. In contrast, the Japanese employees expected and wanted to be told how to do it even better!

Japanese firms that have risen to global leadership over the past decades invariably began with ambitions that were out of all proportion to their resources. One only has to look at how small firms like Canon ('Beat Xerox') and Komatsu ('Encircle Caterpillar') set their sights, not on the immediate competition, but on beating the industry leaders to illustrate this point. They achieved great things by creating an obsession with winning at all levels of the organization. This obsession creates strategic intent. The key focus is on winning, defined in terms of the hardest possible targets. The firms motivate employees by the value of this target. They use the target to develop a long attention span. They are clear about the end point (their strategic 'mission') but flexible as to means, leaving room for individual and team contributions and constantly emphasizing improving competences/skills. They look to develop layers of competitive advantage and do not just focus on one target. For example, they might combine cost-reduction measures with differentiation strategies, expansion of markets and diversification. Their goal is to create new rules of competition. They refuse to play by the existing rules, which are set by industry leaders, because they realize they cannot hope to compete on the leaders' terms. They innovate by leveraging resources to achieve unattainable ends.

In comparison, the emphasis in most Western firms has been on strategic fit. Rather than 'leveraging resources to achieve the impossible', Western firms tend to trim ambition to match available resources. Strategy means positioning according to others' rules, i.e. the rules of dominant firms. All one can hope to achieve by doing this is to project the future forward. With strategic intent, the emphasis is on 'folding the future back', making a future vision a reality by evaluating present actions in terms of how they contribute to the realization of the vision. By playing to the same rules as

## Exhibit 4.5 Japanese success – working from below

In our recent awe of things Japanese, most [Westerners] forget that the original products of the Japanese automotive manufacturers badly missed the mark. Toyota's Toyopet was square, sexless, and mechanically defective. It failed miserably, as did Datsun's first several entries [into Western markets]. More recently, Mazda miscalculated badly with its first rotary engine and nearly went bankrupt. Contrary to myth, the Japanese did not from the onset embark on a strategy to seize the high-quality small car market. They manufactured what they were accustomed to building in Japan and tried to sell it abroad. Their success, as any Japanese automotive executive will readily agree, did not result from a bold insight by a few big brains at the top. On the contrary, success was achieved by senior managers humble enough not to take their initial strategic positions too seriously. What saved Japan's near-failures was the cumulative impact of 'little brains' in the form of salesmen and dealers and production workers, all contributing incrementally to the quality and market positions these companies enjoy today. Middle and upper management saw their primary task as guiding and orchestrating this input from below rather than steering the organization from above along a predetermined course.

The Japanese don't use the term 'strategy' to describe a crisp business definition or competitive master plan. They think more in terms of 'strategic accommodation', or 'adaptive persistence', underscoring their belief that corporate direction evolves from a incremental adjustment to unfolding events. Rarely, in their view, does one leader (or a strategic planning group) produce a bold strategy that guides the firm unerringly. Far more frequently, the input is from below. It is this ability of an organization to move information and ideas from the bottom to the top and back again in continuous dialogue that the Japanese value above all things. As this dialogue is pursued, what in hindsight may be 'strategy' evolves. In sum, 'strategy' is defined as 'all things necessary for the successful functioning of organization as an adaptive mechanism.

*Source*: Pascale (1984: 63–4).

everybody else, Western firms become very predictable and seriously limit their options. Their strategies tend to emphasize buying and selling businesses rather than developing them.

---

### Questions

1. How does your firm welcome and develop its new members?
2. If you had to write a speech to welcome new recruits what would you put in it? Woody Allen's 'My speech to the graduates' begins: 'More than any other time in history, mankind faces a crossroads. One path leads to despair and utter hopelessness. The other, to total extinction. Let us pray we have the wisdom to choose correctly'! It ends: 'We are a people who lack defined goals. We have never learned to love. We lack leaders and coherent programs. We have no spiritual centre. We are adrift alone in the cosmos wreaking monstrous violence on one another out of frustration and pain. Fortunately, we have not lost our sense of proportion. Summing up, it is clear the future holds great opportunities. It also holds pitfalls. The trick will be to avoid pitfalls, seize the opportunities, and get back home by six o'clock.' It is interesting to compare this with Akio Morita's speech to Sony graduates: 'We did not draft you. This is not the army, so that means you have voluntarily chosen Sony. This is your responsibility, and normally if you join this company we expect that you will stay for the next twenty or thirty years. Nobody can live twice, and the next twenty or thirty years is the brightest period of your life. You only get it once. When you leave this company thirty years from now or when your life is finished, I do not want you to regret that you spent all those years here. That would be a tragedy. I cannot stress the point too much that this is your responsibility to yourself. So I say to you, the most important thing in the next few months is for you to decide whether you will be happy or unhappy here' (Morita, 1987: 131–2).
3. Would you say that firms you know demonstrate 'strategic intent'? If *yes*, how? If *no*, what would it need to do to develop it?

## CASE STUDY

Strategic human resource management – Ford Motor Company

'Strategic intent' is not the sole preserve of Far Eastern companies. Leading Western companies such as Ford and IBM have set hard competitive challenges to their employees in the pursuit of new competitive advantage based on quality. Ford is synonymous with the creation of a particular management style – Fordism – based on bureaucratic organization, hierarchical decision-making with strict functional specialization and tightly defined job design and specialized machinery to mass produce a standard product for mass markets. A conjunction of market and technological factors in the 1980s forced Ford to rethink its organization, to redesign jobs and to radically change its culture. The organizational model for its rethinking of its approach to personnel management was, in part, Japanese-inspired. Indeed the major change initiative of Ford of Europe in the early 1980s was called 'After Japan'. The primary impetus to change arose from growing recognition of the magnitude of the Japanese threat, actual in the United States, and imminent in the United Kingdom with the establishment of the Nissan plant in the north-east of England. The new competition posed the threat of radically new standards of efficiency, quality and design. The company had its close links with Mazda, in which it owns a 25 per cent stake, to serve as a source of competitive benchmarking. This benchmarking formed the basis of its long-term strategy.

The major challenge Ford management has set itself is to develop a cooperative employee relations environment to improve its capacity for strategic change. The move is towards cooperative employee relations policies and practices in a firm and industry that has been synonymous with conflictual relations between management and employees. Company strategy is embodied in the 1984 mission statement (see figure 1.6). Ford's mission is to be a worldwide leader in automotive and related products and services, and in newer industries such as financial services. The human resource emphasis is reinforced by the company's value statement: 'Ford's basic values are people, products, and profits', and guiding principles that include 'Employee involvement is our way of life.' The process was facilitated in the United States by the active cooperation of the United

Automobile Workers union, a form of cooperation that was not forthcoming in the United Kingdom.

A key focus of employee and management development at Ford is the 'human resources issue'. All of the company's strategic issues such as quality improvement, customer satisfaction, innovation and cost reduction have one common denominator. They all depend on the capacities, competencies and commitment of Ford employees. The key strategic issue, now and into the future, is how to create and sustain a flexible workforce with the capacities, competencies and commitment (including the technical and managerial leadership) that will give the company a competitive edge in a turbulent, uncertain world marketplace.

At the core of Ford's new human resource management system lie participative management and employee involvement. Participative management is defined as 'the techniques and skills that managers use to provide employees with opportunities to participate actively in key managerial processes affecting job related matters'. Techniques include job redesign, team building, task forces and problem-solving groups. Skills include contracting (establishing clear expectations), rewarding and modelling participative skills. Employee involvement is defined as 'the processes by which employees at all levels have the opportunities to participate actively in the key managerial processes affecting job-related matters'. The processes offering opportunities for participation include consultation (to maximize information and commitment), collaboration (based on a norm of consensus) and delegation (the manager assigns responsibility for an agreed outcome to an individual or group). The joint aim of management and unions is, in the United States at least, to make work a more satisfying experience, improve the overall work environment, enhance creativity, contribute to improvements in the workplace, and help achieve quality, efficiency and reduce absenteeism.

---

## Questions

1. What are the links between strategy and organizational issues in this case?
2. The strategic change initiative described in this case was more successful in the United Kingdom than in the United States. What reasons can you think of to explain this?

3. Does the United Kingdom have particular problems of human resource management that are likely to impact on strategy? If *yes*, what are these problems and how should they be addressed?
4. Is human resource management in your company supportive of strategy? If *yes*, how? If *no*, why not?

---

**Exercise**

Peters and Waterman identified eight successful management practices that led to excellence. These are set out in figure 4.5.

1. Think of an organization that you would class as 'excellent'. List those features that you consider contribute to this excellence. Are these the same features that are emphasized in the Peters and Waterman approach or in the Japanese management system?
2. Think of another organization that you would class as excellent. List those features that you consider contribute to this excellence. Are these the same features that are emphasized in the Peters and Waterman approach or in the Japanese management system?
3. Are the features you found in the first organization the same features that you picked out in the second? If *yes*, you are well on the way to developing your own model of excellence. You will, of course, need a few more examples to complete the picture. If *no*, then you need to consider other organizations until the features start to repeat themselves to form your model.
4. Is your conclusion radically different from Peters and Waterman's and the Japanese model? If *yes*, write a book. You are well on the way to becoming rich and famous!

---

*Magic kingdoms?*

Two examples illustrate the lengths to which management must go to establish excellence. These are two firms commonly acknowledged to provide an unparalleled level of service provision that many others would love to emulate – the Walt Disney Organization, which has recently opened Euro-Disney in France; and Marks & Spencer, acclaimed by many as the United Kingdom's best-managed company.

**A bias for action**
- Project teams that tend to be small, fluid, *ad hoc* and problem/action-focused.
- Communications are of the essence, and there is an important commitment to learning and experimentation.
- Complex problems are tackled through a willingness to shift resources to where they are needed to encourage fluidity and action (chunking).

**Close to the customer**
- The market-driven principle of commitment to service, reliability, and quality, based on an appreciation of 'nichemanship' and the ability to custom-tailor a product or service to a client's needs.

**Autonomy and entrepreneurship**
- A principle which champions innovation, decentralization, the delegation of power and action to the level where they are needed, and a healthy tolerance of failure.

**Productivity through people**
- The principle that employees are people and a major resource, and should be trusted, respected, inspired, and made 'winners'.
- Organizational units should be small-scale to preserve and develop a people-oriented quality.

**Hands-on, value-driven**
- Organization guided by a clear sense of shared values, mission, and identity, relying on inspirational leadership rather than bureaucratic control.

**Stick to the knitting**
- The principle of building on strengths and knowledge of one's niche.

**Simple form, lean staff**
- Avoid bureaucracy; build main commitments to projects or product division rather than to the dual lines of responsibility found in formal matrix organizations; use small organizational units.

**Simultaneous loose–tight properties**
- The principle that reconciles the need for overall control with a commitment to autonomy and entrepreneurship.

**Figure 4.5**  Eight excellent management skills
*Source*: Morgan (1986)

### *Walt Disney*

Walt Disney is one of Peters and Waterman's leading excellent companies and Disney World in Florida provides a model of excellent provision of service to the customer with outstanding value for money. The Magic Kingdom serves over 25 million customers a year, which requires over 25,000 people doing 1,100 different jobs. The quality of service depends on elaborate training to develop employees (though Disney does not use this term) who are committed to their jobs and the organization and deliver consistently high levels of work performance.

New employees receive extensive training in the way Disney is managed and the Disney way of doing things – the Disney philosophy. Individuals are socialized into the Disney tradition. They become 'cast members', *not* employees, whose work is to perform in a show. They wear costumes rather than uniforms. In public – 'on stage' – they perform according to carefully constructed scripts. Visitors to Disney World are 'guests'. Management's main employee relations objectives are to share company goals with employees, to give them a clear, consistent picture of the nature of the work required of them, and to make sure they share and live Disney values (in public at least). The key strategic focus is on quality of service provided by committed and competent staff.

The arrival of Disney in Europe with the opening of Euro-Disney raised many interesting questions. The strategic focus is the same – the provision of a high-quality, value-for-money entertainment experience in a world of make-believe and fun. The major question is whether this American service idea is transferable to Europe. Will Europeans take to the 'Have a nice day' culture and, perhaps, more importantly, will Euro-Disney staff be up to providing service with a smile? (The Magic Kingdom concept has, it should be noted, already been transferred successfully to Japan.)

The President of Euro-Disney argues strongly that Europe presents no special problems and that the levels of service provided by Euro-Disney are already excellent. His view is that it is not national culture that is important as the determinant of organizational behaviour, but rather the values of the company and how successfully it teaches these values to its employees. Press reports on Euro-Disney, however, suggest problems. The *Financial Times* (23 April 1992) suggests that the fair reward for some of the service that it had witnessed was 'confinement in Sleeping Beauty's casket with only Goofy for company'! Disney dismisses these criticisms as teething problems, inevitable in any start-up of this size and complexity. They do not, the company insists, mark a major 'culture shock' issue.

### Marks & Spencer

Marks & Spencer's spectacular success is built upon a strong sense of its values and the fundamental principles it expects its staff to adhere to. These principles include:

(1) to offer our customers a selective range of high-quality, well-designed and attractive merchandise at reasonable prices under the brand name St Michael;

(2) to encourage suppliers to use the most modern and efficient production techniques;

(3) to work with suppliers to ensure highest standards of quality control;

(4) to provide friendly, helpful service and greater shopping comfort and convenience to our customers;

(5) to improve the efficiency of the business, by simplifying operating procedures; and

(6) to foster good human relations with customers, suppliers and staff and in the communities in which we trade.   (Tse, 1985: 9)

Marks & Spencer management has as a major goal the practice of good human relations. They agree with Thomas Watson Jr of IBM that

> There is simply no substitute for good human relations and for the high morale they bring. It takes good people to do the jobs necessary to reach your profit goals. But good people alone are not enough. No matter how good your people may be, if they don't really like the business, if they don't feel totally involved in it, or if they don't think they're being treated fairly – it's awfully hard to get a business off the ground. Good human relations are easy to talk about. The real lesson . . . is that you must work at them all the time and make sure your managers are working with you.   (Tse, 1985: 119)

Remarks made by Marks & Spencer management capture their approach:

> The greatest compliment I can give my staff is to leave them alone to run their own sections.
>
> If you have intelligent, well trained people, you are only wasting your time if you don't let them participate and make decisions with you.
>
> I used to be a manager by setting example, and the staff don't want that. They want to do it themselves. I don't want the board of directors to come and show me what I should do. Provided that they did a good job in training me, I want to go away and execute things myself. The same is true for the staff. They want me to understand them, their hopes and aspirations, but that I let them perform themselves.
>
> The fun for me is not producing the figures that the company wants. I find that fairly easy. The fascination for me is creating a team that automatically produces the figures. And that takes time.   (Tse, 1985: 126)

### Exercise – critical voices

Peters and Waterman's work met with huge success and stimulated great excitement in managerial circles, as did the lessons learnt from the Japanese approach to management. Both approaches, however, have had their critics. Two-thirds of Peters and Waterman's forty-three excellent companies lost their excellence rating five years after the book's publication (Pascale, 1990).

In Search of Excellence has been criticized for sloppy research methodology, poor quality of data and for failing to consider important non-managerial variables such as technology or financial markets. It has been argued that the very variables that made them excellent in the first place planted the seeds for their subsequent decline, that their values were actually myopic and that they were overdependent on unusually charismatic leaders who must eventually burn out. It has also been pointed out that survey evidence suggests that, for people-centred organizations, they were not actually very popular organizations to work for. Some see their management style as manipulative, arguing that people are viewed as instruments of productivity and not valued as individuals in their own right. The same criticism has been levelled at Japanese companies who are accused of driving their employees unmercifully – employees tolerate the pressure imposed on them because they fear losing their jobs and having to leave the core internal labour market with its long-term employment. Japanese firms are also accused of exploiting those who are not part of the internal labour market, their temporary staff and women who never make it to senior positions. Marks & Spencer has been criticized by some for an 'exploitative' attitude to its suppliers, using its power and their relative weakness to negotiate contracts that work very much in Marks's favour.

1. Do you agree or disagree with these criticisms? Give your reasons for agreement or disagreement.
2. Is the Japanese system of management transferable to Western companies?

## Organization design: strategy and structure

We have already mentioned the link between strategy and structure. This is an important link and we will finish off this section by looking at it in more detail. The classic example of how strategy influences structure is the way in which the strategy of diversification led to the development of the multidivisional firm. Changes in strategy led to changes in structure. As we said earlier, the relationship can work in the opposite way. Just as culture can help determine strategic thinking, so an existing structure can affect thinking about strategic options.

Perhaps the most familiar form of organization structure is the *bureaucratic organization*, made up of rigid functional divisions and clearly defined roles and rules with a hierarchical chain of command and control. The multidivisional firm is often made up of a number of bureaucratic sub-units dealing with its different markets. Over recent years the bureaucratic form of organization has been much criticized. Management gurus such as Peter Drucker and Tom Peters have warned that it must radically change if firms are to survive into the twenty-first century. The bureaucracy is criticized for being:

- too hierarchical, thus stifling creativity lower down the organization;
- costly to run, e.g. because of the many managers it needs to try to put into effect its elaborate rules;
- too slow to adapt to increasingly complex and fast-changing environments;
- out of touch with customers – this applies particularly to the strategic apex of senior managers at the top of the hierarchy; and
- demotivating to its employees, who are stifled by the rules and denied the freedom to exercise their creative potential.

Proponents of matrix organizations have tried to balance the functional orientation of the bureaucracy with the priorities of key product and project areas. In the matrix organization, functions are aligned with and balanced by project needs. Rather than abandoning the functional structure, project groups are set up alongside functional departments in a grid or matrix. The matrix structure is thus, in theory, responsive to two managerial needs: the need for strong, specialist functional departments, and the need to be more responsive to the customer whose demands the project is aimed at satisfying, e.g. the need to fine-tune products or services for specific, narrowly defined markets, or the need for products for specific geographic areas. Initially, in the late 1960s and the 1970s, the matrix was seen as the model for the organization of the future. Later it was increasingly criticized as expensive and overelaborate. Critics pointed out that it meant that each individual was answerable to two bosses – thus violating the classical management principle of unity of command – and was a member of at least two potentially competing groups. This can create conflict and confusion. Among the most vociferous critics of the matrix were Peters and Waterman, who argued that the matrix violated one of their cardinal excellent management principles – 'simple form, lean staff'. For Peters and Waterman the major weakness of the matrix is its lack of responsiveness to the need for change. They argue that the matrix virtually always ceases to be innovative, often after just a short while; that it has particular difficulty in executing the basics because the authority structure is weak; and that it also regularly degenerates into anarchy and rapidly becomes bureaucratic and non-creative. The long-term direction of the matrixed organization is usually not clear.

The ideal organization of the future, critics of the bureaucracy and the matrix argue, will be flat, non-hierarchical, 'knowledge-based' and flexible, with highly skilled employees. It will be essentially *project-based*. There may be functional departments but the key organizational unit will be the project team upon whose innovativeness the organization's future depends. In this form of organization, project teams are given the maximum freedom to search for new ideas. Senior management's major role is liaison with the external environment in search of opportunities, contacts and contracts and to publicize the capabilities of its organization. More radical critics of the large, inflexible organization argue that internal reform will never save it and that the organizational form of the future will be the *organic network* operating on a 'small is beautiful' principle with a very small core of staff subcontracting in other skills as and when necessary. The large bureaucratic organization is the result of vertical integration. The organic network is the outcome of vertical disintegration as large firms split themselves up and 'return to basics', concentrating only on their core competence. The fashion industry provides good examples of the network form. A firm like Benetton has created a name and an image, but has a core staff of only around 1,500 people, contracts out its production to a range of small firms and sells through some 2,000 sales points, none of which it owns. One of the roots of Marks & Spencer's success has been its elaborate and dynamic network of suppliers.

Figure 4.6 represents a variant on the organization network theme, the dynamic network, as an illustration of how key tasks can be contracted out.

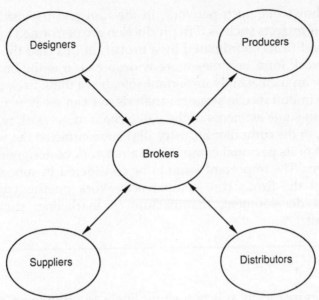

**Figure 4.6** The dynamic network
*Source*: Miles and Snow (1986)

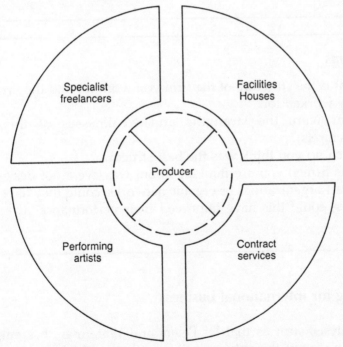

**Figure 4.7** The flexible television/film production company
*Source*: Barnatt and Starkey (1991)

Figure 4.7 shows one such network, in the film and television industry, where one-off projects such as film production are performed by a network of independent firms coordinated by a broker, in this case the producer.

If the network form becomes more widespread, it is the broker who is going to play an increasingly important role. If we think back to the value chain and its importance in strategic analysis, we can see how firms choose to contract out some elements of the value chain in network relationships. For example, in the computer industry IBM subcontracted out work for the development of its personal computer to a network of designers, suppliers and producers. The important issue to be considered in subcontracting is the nature of the firm's core competence. Work on this core, be it in research and development, manufacture or marketing, should not be contracted out.

---

### Exercise

In which industries is subcontracting likely to provide an attractive strategic option? Illustrate your answers with models of the possible networks that might evolve in these industries.

---

### Questions

1. What is the structure of the firm you work for and the firms you have worked for?
2. What were the strengths and weaknesses of this/these structure(s)?
3. Which do you think was the best structure?
4. If the firm(s) you are thinking about was/were not designed as project organizations or organic networks, could they have been? If *yes*, could this have improved their performance? If *no*, why not?

---

## Structuring for international business

Recent analysis, such as that by Peters and Waterman, has emphasized that structure is not the only organizational variable that is important in strategic analysis. Structure and structuring – a broader term that covers the organizational structure issue and how it meshes with the overall management process – are nevertheless still of great importance. Structure and structuring are particularly important as firms grow and they become of crucial strategic concern when firms compete on international grounds.

A central managerial issue that the international firm, the multinational corporation (the MNC) must resolve is the tension between central control and local autonomy. Take the example of Cadbury Schweppes.

> Schweppes Tonic must taste the same, look the same and meet the same quality standards, wherever in the world you order it. This requires the centre to lay down strict quality and presentational guidelines to which the operating units must adhere.
>
> But Tonic is mainly drunk in Britain to make alcohol potable, while next door in France it is drunk as an adult soft drink. The same product is, therefore, consumed for different reasons in the two countries, which in turn means different packaging, different channels of distribution and different customers. Thus the managers on the spot, in charge of each market, have to have the freedom to meet the needs of their particular market place. All large enterprises wrestle with the balance between control from the centre and the ability to respond speedily in the market place. The aim in a branded business is to combine the maximum operating freedom with maintaining a clear worldwide identity for international brands. (Cadbury, 1991: 10)

The single most important organizational question for the MNC is, therefore, the degree of decentralization that is most appropriate to its strategic concerns. There have historically been three answers to this question according to the 'state of the art' study of the issue, Bartlett and Ghoshal's *Managing Across Borders* (1989). They describe these as multinational companies (the typical European structure and management approach developed before World War II), international companies (the approach developed by American MNCs after World War II) and global companies (the Japanese response of the 1970s and 1980s). (Bartlett and Ghoshal's use of the term 'multinational' is rather confusing unless you remember that they use it to describe one particular strategic response, whereas others use it as a generic term to describe the full range of companies competing internationally regardless of their structure and management approach.)

The key strategic strength of the *multinational*, according to Bartlett and Ghoshal, is its ability to build strong local presence through sensitivity and responsiveness to national differences in demand. Many key assets, responsibilities and decisions are decentralized in this approach. Each national subsidiary is given a high degree of independence for strategic and operational decisions. Management regards overseas operations as a portfolio of independent businesses.

The *international* organization adopts a different approach. Its key strength is its ability to exploit parent company knowledge and capabilities through worldwide diffusion and modest adaptation. The US base acts as the source of new product and process knowledge. Management regards overseas operations as appendages to a central, domestic operation. Many assets, resources, responsibilities and decisions are decentralized but decision-making has to be ratified by, and is therefore still controlled by, the centre. A key source of competitive advantage is technology transfer (product or process) from the centre to subsidiaries.

The *global* company, again, is very different from the other two. Its main strength is the ability to build cost advantages through centralized, global-scale operations. Most strategic assets, resources, responsibilities and decisions are centralized with tight central control of decisions, resources and information. Management treats overseas operations as merely delivery pipelines to a unified global market. Hence, the criticism of Japanese investment in the United Kingdom that it is only in manufacture, in 'screwdriver' assembly plants; the strategic and product development work is all done in Japan.

Each of these forms of organization has its own strengths. Each thrives in particular market conditions: the *multinational* form in markets that demand local sensitivity and responsiveness to a variety of demand at the local level; the *international* when the key source of competitive advantage is the transfer of knowledge with broad applications; the *global* when the key industry issue is global efficiency. Changing conditions of global competition, however, demand a new form of organization, according to Bartlett and Ghoshal – the *transnational*. The key strategic issues now encompass both global efficiency and responsiveness to the increasing variety of local conditions. The transnational demonstrates global competitiveness, multinational flexibility and worldwide learning. Its assets, resources, responsibilities and decisions are dispersed *and* interdependent, subsidiaries are given specific roles according to their special competences, and there is joint development and worldwide sharing of learning. The key management tasks include the legitimization and balancing of diverse perspectives, the development of multiple and flexible coordinating processes and the building of individual commitment in pursuit of a shared vision.

The transnational provides

- global integration;
- local differentiation; and
- worldwide innovation.

To enable it to do this it has a range of novel features.

> Each national unit is a source of ideas, skills and capabilities that can be harnessed for the benefit of the total organization.
>
> National units achieve global scale by making them the company's world source for a particular product, component or activity.
>
> The center [establishes] a new, highly-complex managing role which coordinates relationships between units but does so in a highly-flexible way. The key is to focus less on managing activities directly and more upon creating an organizational context which is conducive to the coordination and the resolution of differences. (Grant, 1991: 298)

Creating the right organizational context involves 'establishing clear corporate objectives, developing managers with broadly-based perspec-

**Dominant strategic requirements of industry**

| Responsiveness (branded packaged products) | Unilever | Kao | Procter & Gamble |
|---|---|---|---|
| Efficiency (consumer electronics | Philips | Matsushita | General Electric |
| Transfer of knowledge (telecommunications switching) | ITT | NEC | Ericsson |
| | Responsiveness (multinational) | Efficiency (global) | Transfer of knowledge and competencies (international) |

**Dominant strategic capability of company**

**Figure 4.8**  Industry requirements and company capabilities
*Source*: Bartlett and Ghoshal (1989)

tives and relationships, and fostering supportive organizational norms and values' (Bartlett and Ghoshal, 1989: 388).

Figure 4.8 gives examples of very successful multinational (Unilever), global (Matsushita) and international (Ericsson) firms, together with the characteristics of their industries. The other firms in figure 4.8 are less successful because there is a lack of fit between their dominant strategic capability and the dominant strategic requirements of their industry. For example, Kao, a Japanese consumer goods company similar to Proctor & Gamble, has failed, as yet, to develop on the international stage, despite being very successful in Japan. Kao's strength is global efficiency, based on standardized products, but its market demands local responsiveness. In this industry the multinational, Unilever, has been best suited to this strategic requirement.

---

### Exercise

Devise your own figure using the same axes as figure 4.8 but choosing different firms.

It has been suggested that ICI, Sony and BOC are excellent examples of the transnational. Do you agree? Can you think of other firms that fit the bill?

---

## Strategy, culture and organization

Traditionally, the emphasis in strategy has tended to fall on competition. In an increasing number of industries – such as automobiles and computers – there is a new emphasis on cooperation and various forms of joint venturing between erstwhile head-on competitors. Figure 4.9 summarizes strategic alliances in the automobile industry.

Having suffered a major setback in the videocassette recorder (VCR) market with its attempts to develop its Betamax format as an industry standard, Sony has, in recent R&D activity, focused on joint ventures with apparent competitors. One such joint venture was with Philips in the development of the compact disc. Philips had suffered, like Sony, in the VCR format battle. The logic of the joint venture is to safeguard both parties against the risks of another such failure. The strategic goal of such ventures is to develop jointly a standard of product specification that

| Company | Own equity in | Joint design with | Supply vehicles to | Supply components to | Commercial agreement with |
|---|---|---|---|---|---|
| Chrysler | Mitsubishi 12% | Mitsubishi Renault | Mitsubishi (US) | Fiat (Teksid) | Fiat Honda |
| Daimler–Benz | | | | | Mitsubishi |
| Fiat | | Ford (CVT) | Nissan (SA) Subaru | Subaru | Chrysler |
| Ford | Jaguar 51% Mazda 25% | Mazda (Escort) Nissan (Engine) Fiat (CVT) | VAG (Autolatina) | KIA Korea Mazda | |
| General Motors | Suzuki 5% Daewoo 33% Isuzu 39% Saab 50% | Isuzu (Piazza) | Isuzu (Bedford) Toyota (NUMMI) | Isuzu | |
| Honda | Rover 20% | Rover | | Rover | Chrysler |
| Isuzu | | GM | GM Subaru (Indiana) | | |
| Mazda | KIA 8% | Ford | KIA | Ford | Saab |
| Mitsubishi | Hyundai 15% | Chrysler | Hyundai Chrysler | Hyundai | Volvo Daimler–Benz |
| Nissan | | Ford | Fiat (SA) VAG (Santana) | | |
| PSA | | Renault/Volvo (V6) | | Rover (R65) | Suzuki |
| Renault | Volvo 25% | Volvo (Trucks) PSA/Volvo (V6) Chrysler | | Volvo Subaru (engines) | |
| Rover | Honda UK 20% | Honda | Honda (Concerto) | | |
| Saab | | | | | Mazda |
| Toyota | Daihatsu 15% | Daihatsu | GM (NUMMI) | Daihatsu | |
| VAG | Seat 50% | | Ford (Autolatina) Toyota (Hilux) | | |
| Volvo | Renault 20% | Renault/PSA (V6) | | | Mitsubishi |

**Figure 4.9** A summary of alliances between automotive manufacturers
*Source*: Pilkington (1991)

dominates a particular television market. When the standard is accepted the development partners can again become competitors but only in manufacturing, using the same industry standard. Both thus safeguard their R&D investment. In this way the two firms guard against the certainty of one losing heavily if they had pursued individual developments.

One of the most interesting joint ventures of recent years has been in the computer industry between Apple and IBM. Let us examine this from Apple's point of view. Apple is the relative newcomer to the industry; IBM the old, established global giant. Apple has focused on the high value-added end of the personal computer market but has experienced major problems in building market share, particularly in the large business user market. It is now changing its strategy to go for market share through introducing cut-price 'bread and butter' versions of its highly regarded Macintosh product. The new emphasis on market share follows the marketing-led changes introduced into the company by John Sculley, formerly of Pepsi Co., who in a bitter boardroom battle ousted the charismatic founder of the company, Steve Jobs. Jobs, the board concluded, had clung for too long to his vision of Apple as being quintessentially concerned with technological innovation at the expense of the bottom line. Sculley convinced the board that this was the primrose path to oblivion.

Sculley explains the business imperatives as follows:

> We looked at ourselves in the mirror and wondered if we had a justifiable business strategy for the 1990s. Our model was one of high margins with huge product differentiation. But growth was slowing. Computers were becoming more of a commodity.   (*Fortune*, 4 May 1992)

As part of the new business approach, as opposed to the existing emphasis on technology in the company, Sculley led Apple into a strategic alliance with its former arch-enemy, IBM, to pursue the innovations Apple felt it no longer had the resources to pursue alone. IBM's potential gain in this venture is to tap into Apple's undoubted technological expertise and exciting product developments, particularly in software that make computers easy to use ('user-friendly'). A major attraction for Apple is the route IBM provides into the lucrative business market. Analysts argue, however, that the new demands of the joint venture will present major problems for Apple's famed entrepreneurial culture and even threaten the very 'soul' of the company.

> A lingering question: How will Apple's new way of doing business affect the special qualities that inform the company's culture? Employee after employee extols 'Apple magic.' They speak of the sense of empowerment felt by almost

everyone who works there, and say that even lower-level workers on a development team can delay release of a product if they don't think it is ready. The good feeling is palpable in the relaxed atmosphere and easygoing enthusiasm that fills the headquarters in Cupertino.

[The Head of Apple's advanced technology group], for one, doesn't think the IBM alliance will change this sensibility. 'When we get together with the IBM guys, they look more like Apple people than we do like IBM people. Culturally, IBM will be moving a lot closer to Apple.' But Sculley sounds like an IBMer when he summarizes the reasons for his new strategy: 'Our cost structure was out of line. We didn't know how to meet schedules. We were a benevolent company that sponsored people to work on things they were interested in.'   (*Fortune*, 4 May 1992)

---

### Discussion point

Analysts argue that joint ventures are very difficult to maintain and that they usually work (or are exploited) to the advantage of only one of the partners. Need this necessarily be the case?

# 5 The management of strategic change

The reality of life is that while staying put is without doubt the most comfortable for the short haul, it is in fact the highest risk strategy of all. Sadly, one can see example after example where the company or the individual who was leading the race believed that they had found the ultimate solution and stayed with it too long, while somebody else was stimulated to greater effort and overtook. . . . The world of industry is one of perpetual change not only technologically, but also as a part of the continuous ferment of the developing universe in which we live. . . . By and large in an industrial organization one's people should be asking not whether you are going to change, but how long it will be before you do. Wait too long and you have lost control, move too soon and you will lack the commitment which is vital to success. (Harvey-Jones, 1989: 127–8)

## Triggers for change

Strategic management is concerned with the long-term health of a business. In many ways it is about creating predictability in the firm's relationship to its environment – an environment that is increasingly in flux – and stability in the organization in terms of its goals, policies and programmes. (Remember the strategy hierarchy in chapter 1.) But strategic management is also about monitoring one's present way of proceeding and deciding when that is no longer adequate. Strategic management is, therefore, often concerned with the management of change. Managers need to be aware of when change is necessary. Indeed a major aspect of the techniques and concepts we have been addressing in the previous chapters has been an attempt to sensitize the reader to the need for constant strategic vigilance and evaluation. When this vigilance and evaluation suggest that the objectives of the business or the major plans and policies are no longer appropriate, or that the results of implementing the strategy do not confirm their critical assumptions, then is the time to change. The strategy may have become inconsistent (objectives and policies might no longer complement each other), it may have lost consonance (it is no longer responsive to important environmental changes), it may no longer generate advantage (the firm is losing its basis for competitive advantage), or it may no longer be feasible (there are no longer the resources to implement it).

Triggers for change are many and various. The environment might become more complex and less predictable. Market change as consumers demand different products or services might render your offerings less attractive. The effect of Japanese products on consumer demands in the automobile, motorcycle and audio-visual consumer products industries are good examples of such a change. Competitors might come up with a radical innovation in technology that demands a total rethink of your technological base, both in terms of new product technologies and new production process. Pilkington's breakthrough in making float glass is a good example here. It set the standards of competition for decades to come in the glass industry and meant that competitors had to get their production know-how on licence from Pilkington. Pilkington thus managed to dominate its industry. Change in the politics of the organization can occur when there is disagreement about the future mission of the organization or the way in which the organization is structured or about best modes of manufacture. The arrival of new top management can lead to change as the balance of power over decision-making shifts. We have already referred to the effect of Harvey-Jones's new vision at ICI. One can also think of the effect of Michael Edwardes at British Leyland or Lee Iacocca at Chrysler. Such new arrivals lead to a political problem in the sense that the organization has to determine who has the power to decide on what course of action. This can lead to major changes in the culture of the organization and fundamental changes in its set of core beliefs and values. Top management has to determine what values need to be held by which people.

## Radical change

Figure 5.1 sets out a model of the strategic change process. There are two views of how successful strategic change needs to be managed. One argues in favour of radical revolutionary change, the need to sweep away the past to leave the stage clear for the new and radically different. The second view argues that change should be managed incrementally as a series of small gradual steps. We will consider the radical view first.

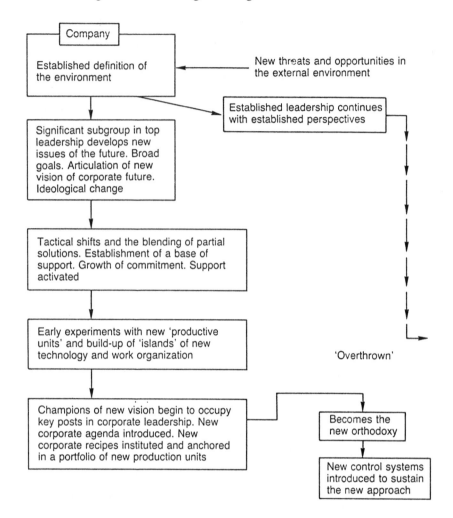

**Figure 5.1**    Implementing strategic change
*Source*: Derived from Quinn (1980)

Radical change comes about as a result of the development of concern about the firm's current situation on the part of a subgroup of people in the organization. There may be a precipitating critical event. The subgroup with its new vision of the organization needs to assume a position of power to get its understanding of the problems facing the organization accepted. In this process the old guard of top managers moves aside or is replaced. New objectives are set and new plans devised. The new strategy is then implemented and the changes stabilized. Change, according to this approach, tends to be dramatic, occurring in quantum leaps. If managed

---

### Exhibit 5.1    Strategic change at ICI in the 1980s

Change at ICI over this period was not continuous and incremental. It took place as a series of radical and revolutionary packages interspersed with periods of incremental adjustment. Change included rationalization and retrenchment in some sectors and also fundamental, revolutionary changes in thinking about the balance of ICI products and spread of geographical interests. There was a move from heavy to speciality chemicals and geographical repositioning of markets from the United Kingdom to the United States and, later, the Pacific Basin. Changes in core beliefs about the nature of the business led to major changes in business strategy and in organizational structure and management systems. The radical changes were associated with changes in leadership.

*Source*: Pettigrew (1985).

---

well, its supporters argue, radical change is more effective than a piecemeal approach in which change is introduced gradually in an incremental fashion. The radical approach leads to quantum leaps in strategy, which means that organizations make clean, clear breaks with the past and move from one strategy to another without a long transition through a variety of interim stages where future direction is not clear. Customers and employees thus know exactly where they stand.

## The incremental approach to change

The alternative view of change is that it should be managed in a far more gradual, incremental way. Supporters of this approach argue that the strategy process is extremely complex. Managers need, therefore, to proceed cautiously. They also need time to explore the complexities facing their organization, to experiment with different strategies and to judge between a range of options. According to Quinn (1980), a leading proponent of theories of incrementalism, the processes used to arrive at a strategy are typically fragmented, evolutionary and largely intuitive. Their roots lie deep in top managers' minds and their rationality is, thus, difficult to assess. Pieces of formal strategic analysis do contribute to the final strategy – but only pieces. In the final analysis strategy tends to *evolve* as internal decisions and external events come together in the minds of managers, whose task is then to create a new, widely shared consensus for action. Far from being an abrogation of good management practice, Quinn argues, the rationale behind this kind of strategy formulation is so powerful that it perhaps provides the normative model for strategic decision-making – rather than the step-by-step 'formal systems planning' approach so often espoused.

Incrementalism makes good strategic sense. Early commitments are kept relatively open and subject to review. Change programmes and their planning develop in phases or stages with concrete decisions to proceed further taken only at the end of each phase, say of new product development. Final commitments are postponed until the last possible moment. The rationale for proceeding in this way is that the full implications of alternative actions need to be explored. The organization's capability for alternative actions also needs to be explored. Top management needs to sense what their employees are capable of. Top management also needs to be sensitive to the politics of the organization, to create awareness of the need for change and to involve everybody in mobilizing the organization's resources for change. Top management also needs to test the inputs of various groups into the strategy process and to give people the opportunity to learn from and to adapt to the responses of others. Well-managed interaction between opposing alternatives improves the quality of the final decision and builds commitment to that decision, even among groups whose initiatives are finally unsuccessful. The environment also needs to be explored in the sense that managers need to be as sure as possible of the direction of external change. New products are never justified by analysis. In the final analysis major changes are a matter of faith.

Incrementalism, therefore, should be conscious. Managers should accept the cognitive and process limits on each major change decision, while at the same time striving to build a logical-analytical framework in which to take decisions.

The success of incrementalism also depends upon top management's ability to create the awareness, understanding, acceptance and commitment needed to implement strategies effectively.

## Radical and incremental change compared

The alert reader will by now be asking whether or not the radical and the incremental approaches to change contradict each other. The answer is: not necessarily. It depends what you focus on. The incremental view focuses on the processes going on in the strategists' minds and the interactive way in which they manage their organizations to generate information and commitment. The radical change view focuses not on processes but on the actual content of strategic change, the realized strategies of the organization. These generally seem to change in a kind of quantum leap, particulary when viewed 'objectively' from the outside. But to achieve this apparent speed of transition that can so bedazzle competitors and business analysts when it is effective, managers might well have had to pursue the long, slow path of incrementalism to change people's minds within their organization, to sell the new ideas and to harness the effort to make the 'quantum leap' possible.

---

### Question

Have you had experience of a major change in an organization you have worked for or dealt with? Was this change managed in a radical or incremental manner? If you have had experience of both radical and incremental change, which do you consider most effective?

---

## Strategy subsystems

The management of strategic change is improved by applying incremental logic to the various elements of the change decision. Quinn (1980) suggests that we think of these elements as subsystems (figure 5.2). The successful management of change depends upon management's ability to focus strategic thinking by making the subsystems the object of ongoing analysis.

If we analyse the workings of some of these subsystems we can appreciate better why they benefit from incremental management. The *acquisition/diversification subsystem*, as the name suggests, is concerned with strategic decisions concerning diversification through either internal

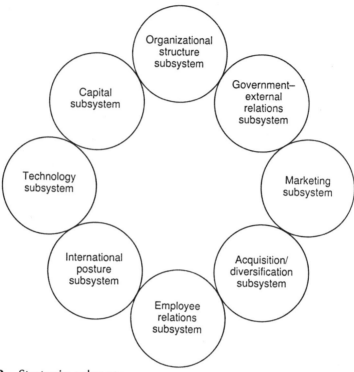

**Figure 5.2**   Strategic subsystems
*Source*: Adapted from Quinn (1980)

development or external acquisition. An incremental approach is necessary to investigate options and prepare the way for internal or external diversification. Top management needs to manage skilfully the politics of such major changes, to create consensus concerning the need for change, and to develop commitment to new programs of action. A 'comfort factor for risk-taking' needs to be established, which might necessitate changing the value-system of the organization and various subsystems, e.g. the capital subsystem centred on the finance department if (!) its attitudes are anti-risk. The organization has to be prepared to move opportunistically to take advantage of opportunities. The other side of the coin of diversification is divestment, and the same preparatory work is necessary to manage this successfully. The psychological effects of pulling out of what might have been core businesses should not be underestimated and they certainly have to be prepared for if they are not to prove disruptive, e.g. by demotivating people who feel their area might be next to go.

Diversification might require major reorganization and thus impact on the *organizational structure subsystem*. Diversification might be accompanied by decentralization, in which case staff manning the decentralized units will have to be prepared for this responsibility and staff at the centre will have to come to terms with a consequent loss of power. New roles thus created have to be carefully thought through in all their detail, e.g. in terms of how they affect individual career goals and the timing of individual career moves. While decentralized participative structures encourage new ideas, they can also make it difficult actually to implement any of them. The actual implementation of the change idea fostered by devolving more responsibility for ideas might need more centralized, more tightly controlled structures.

Major reorganization has to be managed incrementally as its inevitable unexpected results become clear. When Exxon began to decentralize on a worldwide basis, the Executive Committee allocated a board member with a participative management style to what they vaguely termed a 'coordinative role' to deal with the problems of decentralization in Europe. Over a period of two years this man diagnosed problems and experimented with various coordination solutions to develop greater understanding of the complex issues involved by both corporate and divisional managers. Finally, now aware of the problems and able to deal with them, Exxon moved to a more formal 'line' relationship with what became Exxon Europe. Similar processes were adopted in other areas of the world. All of these changes together led to an entirely new internal power balance between the corporate centre and the regional organizations and to a more responsive worldwide posture for Exxon (Quinn, 1980).

Logical incrementalism links together information gathering, analysis, testing of options, and the behavioural and political aspects of the strategic subsystems. Firms will explore a variety of options in the technology subsystem before deciding upon one product or process technology. They will also explore a variety of product positioning options before deciding upon one strategy for the marketing subsystem. By organizing its approach to strategic decision-making using subsystems, top management can:

- generate better communications by bringing together representatives of the subsystems for interactive discussion;
- involve lower levels of the organization to the benefit of maximizing relevant information-gathering;
- help generate commitment by disseminating information about the strategic issues facing the firm and how they impact upon the subsystems and the people in them; and
- keep the future to the forefront of managers' attention so that they do not become buried under the day-to-day hue and cry.

Of crucial importance in the strategy process is the recognition that the various subsystems interact: the ramifications of decisions in one area for other areas have to be explored. For example, a major change in product technology is likely to require changes in production technology. This will affect marketing, and is likely to affect the organization structure. Capital will obviously be an important issue in the new investment required. And so on . . . For example, IBM's decision to invest in the production of a new family of computers using a new technology made obsolete a number of existing products manufactured in different divisions whose product lines were anyway beginning to overlap. Rationalization of the activities of these other divisions in one new division was considered appropriate. This also focused the whole organization's effort on making the new 'make or break' initiative work.

One ignores the interaction of subsystems at one's peril. One way of thinking about Michael Edwardes's efforts to turn around British Leyland is that he concentrated too much on one subsystem – employee relations – at the expense of marketing and technology. Thus he largely sorted out the industrial relations problems that had bedevilled the company in the 1970s, but he failed to generate new products to do well in core markets and made some bad decisions concerning investment in the technology of new manufacturing systems. The best employees in the world cannot perform competitively if they do not have a good product to make and if they have the wrong production system. Subsystems need to balance and complement each other.

---

### Question

What are the key subsystems in your organization? Trace through the ramifications of decisions in one subsystem on others. What is the major subsystem at the moment. Why?

---

## Managing change

Typically you start with a general concern, vaguely felt. Next, you roll an issue around in your mind until you think you have a conclusion that makes sense for the company. Then you go out and sort of post the idea without being too wedded to its details. You then start hearing the arguments pro and con, and some very good refinements of the idea usually emerge. Then you pull the idea in and put some resources together to study it so it can be put forward as more of a formal presentation. You wait for 'stimuli occurrences' or 'crises,' launch pieces of the idea to help in these situations. But they lead toward your ultimate aim. You know where you want to get. You'd like to get there in six months. But it may take three years, or you may not get there at all. And when you do get there, you don't know whether it was originally your own idea – or somebody else had reached the same conclusion before you and you just got on board for it. You never know.   (senior executive, quoted by Quinn, Mintzberg and James, 1988: 671)

Change tends to be easier in small, innovative organizations than larger, complex ones. Small entrepreneurial companies possess the following characteristics:

- *Need orientation* – entrepreneurs have a strong need to achieve. They tend to be fanatical in their desire to succeed and to establish their companies as going concerns.
- *Flexibility and quickness* – their simple structures and a management process dominated by founder figures make them quick to react to market signals and to adapt their product accordingly.
- *Strong incentives* – entrepreneurs are clear that there are significant rewards available if they are successful in getting their ideas to market.

In the United States, more than in the United Kingdom, entrepreneurs also have ready access to capital through a variety of sources such as venture capitalists ready and willing to finance likely ideas.

Large companies, in contrast, experience major barriers to innovation. Top management tends to become remote from both the market place and those people lower down the company with good ideas (the 'intrapreneurs'). Indeed they often see people who have new ideas as 'troublemakers', ready to rock the boat. They do not promote incentives to foster innovation. They also tend to become risk-averse as they proceed up the career ladder. Their decisions are dominated by short time horizons, linked to the constraints of accounting practices and the workings of the financial markets. Bureaucratic rules tend to dominate and these, by their very definition, are meant to safeguard the status quo.

Yet some large companies have found the secret of innovation. These companies are characterized by the following:

- *Atmosphere and vision* – top management value innovation and manage their company culture to support it. Sony's policy on this is a shining example – the company goal is for motivated individuals to exercise their technological skills to the highest level.

- *Orientation to the market* – there is a strong focus on the customer, exemplified in the case of Sony by technical people having to spend time in learning marketing skills.
- *Small, flat organizations* – with fewer management levels between the innovators ('intrapreneurs') and top management and a minimum of bureaucratic constraints on project teams. There are only short decision lines between the champions of new ideas and the top-level decision-makers, thus reducing response time.
- *Concentrating on a few key thrusts* – top managers focus attention and effort on a limited range of options (six to ten) that integrate the firm's existing and newly emerging concerns.
- *Developmental 'shootouts'* – a variety of groups might work on solutions to different problems. The groups are pitted against each other to ensure that the best solution to the problem emerges from the multiple approaches. Such interactions between different teams encourage learning from each other. Top management has to foster a spirit of 'win-win' competition rather than 'zero sum' games where one team wins at the expense of another (Quinn, 1980).

In these innovating organizations the emphasis is on 'means strategies' rather than 'ends strategies'. Strategic leadership is less concerned with formulating and implementing strategy in the traditional sense than with establishing the behavioural processes within the organization that will ensure new strategies emerge. The strategist is responsible for managing the process rather than the content. To manage this process is not to preconceive strategy but to recognize when a viable strategy has emerged, and then to step in and ensure that it is taken up by others in the organization to ensure its success. The strategy then becomes deliberate. During the course of its lifecycle, top management must be looking to the processes that will encourage the emergence of the strategies of the future that will replace the current strategy, thus creating a virtuous circle of strategy renewal.

Quinn (1980) argues that the value of a strategy lies not in its clarity or in the rigid adherence to its plan. Rather a strategy is valuable to the extent that it succeeds in 'capturing the initiative' in the sense of helping the organization to deal with essentially unpredictable events, to redeploy and concentrate resources as new opportunities and thrusts emerge, and thus to use resources most effectively towards selected goals. The strategy sets clear goals but is flexible as to means. Successful managers who operate logically and proactively in an incremental mode become successful by building understanding, identity and commitment through the actual processes through which the strategies are created. Incrementalism allows them to improve the quality of information used in decisions, generated through the incremental management of subsystems, and to deal with the politics of change – i.e. the sensitive management of differences among interested parties – while they build, step by step, the organization's momentum toward the new strategy and generate the psychological motivation to carry it through.

## The innovating organization

Some organizations exist in industries where survival depends on innovation – the fashion or film industries with their constant search for the new are good examples. Most businesses, however, do not have this total preoccupation with fickle fashion and with novelty. All organizations nevertheless do need to be aware of innovation as a strategic weapon. Many successful firms have run into difficulties because they refused to consider the possibility of change. It was said of Henry Ford, for example – one of the most influential inventors and business men in history – that 'the old master failed to master change'. He developed an incredibly successful product – the Model T motor car, any colour so long as it was black – and the organization to ensure its smooth production. But he lacked the strategic vision to see that, in time, consumer taste would change and a one-dimensional product would no longer satisfy it (see chapter 3).

It is possible to design an organization for innovation. Such an innovating organization's design characteristics are depicted in figure 5.3. The task of the organization or subunit of the organization – innovation – is defined by the strategic concerns at its particular stage of development. Innovation needs key roles. You need the people with ideas, the idea generators, and you also need people to champion (sponsor) ideas at a higher level so they get onto the strategic agenda. The generators are not necessarily the best managers of projects. You need orchestrators to make sure the ideas are implemented. You need a management process that will generate ideas, move from the old to the new (transitioning) and put the new idea into practice. You need rewards for people involved in innovation, both the idea generators, the sponsors and also the orchestrators. Rewards include the intrinsic satisfaction of autonomy, the freedom to be creative, recognition, perhaps by promotion, and financial

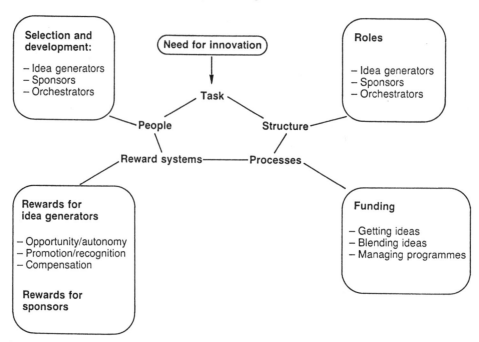

**Figure 5.3**   Designing innovating organizations
*Source*: Adapted from Galbraith and Kazanjian (1986)

rewards. The organization needs to select and develop the people who are going to occupy these key roles.

The ideal situation for a firm, as has already been mentioned, is to have a range of products, some strong in their markets (the cash cows), others with great potential for the future in fast-growing markets (the 'rising stars', stars of the future). Such a firm has a dual core, one based on its current mainstay businesses, the other geared to innovation. The innovatory unit/division can be structured along the lines just described as conducive to innovation; the business that has reached its potential in a reasonably stable industry can be structured in a different way, more along bureaucratic lines, though with the major excesses of the bureaucracy removed. Top management's role in the latter is to fine-tune the business because the strategy that has gained the unit its success is still viable. There is an accepted industry recipe for success. Pilkington provides a good example of such an organization (figure 5.4). Some of Pilkington's divisions, such as Flat Glass and Glass Fibre, are operating in mature markets and are structured primarily for efficiency. In other divisions, such as Electro-optical, innovation is the key and this division is structured as a set of small innovatory units with high levels of autonomy to facilitate the

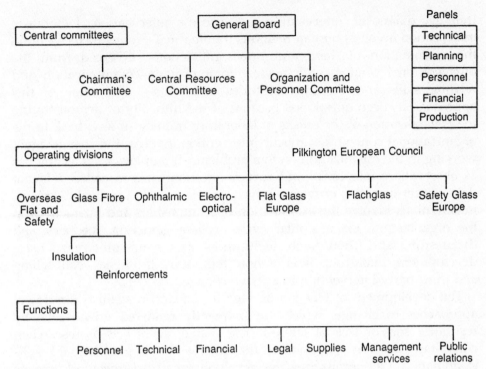

**Figure 5.4** Pilkington Brothers plc– organization structure
*Source*: Company records

maximum levels of new discovery. The long-term aim of the company is to grow the newer units to a larger proportion of their corporate portfolio to offset diminishing returns from traditional businesses in the future.

## Organizational development and strategy

It is wrong to equate reorganization with change, though restructuring can form an important part of strategic change. For real change to occur, structural change must be accompanied by individual attitude changes. Organization development (OD) provides a source of knowledge and techniques to improve an organization's strategic capability through improving its problem-solving and renewal processes, particularly through a more effective and collaborative management of organization culture based on the development of work teams, with the assistance of a change agent, either from inside or outside the organization (a consultant), as catalyst. There are three broad categories of OD approach: laboratory training, diagnostic intervention and process intervention. Laboratory intervention involves human relations training in T-groups focusing upon the examination of 'here and now' interactions, divorced from the organizational context, with a view to improving communication and relating skills and changing attitudes and values. The value of this approach has been questioned because of the difficulty of demonstrating the generalization of the effects of laboratory training (if any) back to the organizational context. Diagnostic intervention involves the change agent working in the organization on live problems. It employs such techniques as observation, interviews and survey questionnaires to collect relevant data concerning the problem, which are fed back to clients. Process interventions involve the examination of relationships and interactions in the organization, via a similar cycle of data gathering, feedback and discussion, and then such techniques as group meetings, team development, intergroup intervention, temporary taskforces, counselling and third-party intervention to achieve change.

The development of OD can be seen as a reaction against 'top-down' approaches to change, which are frequently rendered unworkable by resistance and/or lack of interest. The change agent acts as researcher, consultant and/or catalyst in the process of organizational self-examination. OD emphasizes the development of existing work groups through collaboration and participation as methods for achieving ownership of change. This follows the view that the focus of change should be the individual in his or her social group and not the individual in isolation. The key unit of change, therefore, is deemed to be the social group from which the individual derives his or her values. OD's early emphasis on social skills and personal and interpersonal processes as an end in itself has been found wanting. It is not enough merely to get people talking and listening to each other effectively. The purpose of improving communication, a major aim in many OD initiatives, is to improve the efficiency of the organization. This requires an understanding of the technology and tasks of the organization and the role of the groups under development. OD has as its goal the harmonization of people, groups, tasks, technology and structures. Early variants of OD have also been criticized for their failure to confront problems of power and interest as key issues in organization change. The change agent has to be aware of organizational politics.

The sequence of an OD intervention is typically as follows:

1. initial consultation to explore the change issue with the internal 'champions' of the need for change;

2.  agreement on the design of the change intervention;
3.  collection, feedback and analysis of relevant data;
4.  intervention planning; and
5.  change initiative.

This sequence may be repeated many times during the course of an intervention. The consultant provides process guidance to facilitate the analysis of data and problem-solving, helping to define the strategies available to the organization.

   An OD initiative aimed at improving the strategy process might proceed as follows:

1.  Champions initiate change intervention.
2.  Analysis of change issue while learning the skills (vocabulary and action principles) necessary to support change initiative. Typically, small groups of managers from different parts and levels of the company will meet to learn the necessary skills and to analyse what needs to be done. Their own strategic leadership style will generally come under the microscope. An open climate is encouraged at this stage. There is a growing consensus that this process should start with the top management group and then cascade down through the organization with feedback going three ways, vertically up and down, and laterally.
3.  A team development phase in which actual work groups focus on how they function. Again this ideally starts with the top group, and openness and trust are encouraged.
4.  An intergroup development phase in which groups that have important working relationships come together, e.g. groups from different functions, to explore how to improve relationships.
5.  Having radically improved the quality of information- and ideas-sharing in the organization, top management is now in a position to develop a strategy for the organization.
6.  The strategy is implemented.
7.  The strategy is evaluated and refined in the light of unfolding events, both internal, as the OD process evolves, and external, as the environment alters.

Using OD, organizations are designed and redesigned (changed) according to the information needs of tasks and the interdependence of tasks. Related to these core problems are issues of organizational process – communication, control, problem-solving and decision-making, reward systems and conflict management. Management has to design communication procedures that minimize distortion, provide timely information, and see that the organization has sufficient openness to facilitate upward and downward communication. Management has to design structures appropriate to the problems facing the organization. More complex problems require more open structures. Less complex problems can be solved with centralized information networks. Appropriate control mechanisms have to be designed with the participation of those involved and control measurements made explicit and realistic. All OD theorists agree that OD involves a long timescale, usually a minimum of two to three years.

## Change in service environments

The problem of change is as great in service as in manufacturing industries. Increasingly, differentiation and diversified product ranges in services give rise to new managerial challenges. A recent survey of personal financial service firms highlighted the need for new specialist skills to deal with new specialized products; new training and recruitment to support these products and develop these skills; and the need for a new type of top manager with a more strategic perspective geared to dealing with the increasing complexity of strategic choices in the industry. To find managers with these new skills it may be necessary to search outside the confines of the industry.

One of the most spectacular banking turnarounds of the 1980s was that of the Bank of Ireland spearheaded by Mark Hely Hutchinson, whom the bank recruited from Guinness. The new chairman brought to the company important new skills in managing a diversified product range and in becoming marketing-led, providing services responsive to customer need. Marketing has been a low priority until recently in financial services. Bank of Ireland advertised aggressively for new customers, particularly young ones, and its outlets were redesigned as 'selling machines' with bottom-line profitability the key measure of all the bank's activities. More flexible organizational structures were introduced with the introduction of a business unit type of organization and the devolution of decision-making to the managers closest to the market. In other service industries major change has necessitated the introduction of new types of managers, i.e. managers with a different industry perspective. In the National Health Service, for example, the Griffiths Report highlighted the lessons to be learnt in health care from the successful management of supermarkets.

(The author of the report was himself from Sainsbury's.) Recent recruitment of NHS management has attempted to bring in people from non-health-related sectors.

### Changing a hospital

1. *External analysis* – agree on summary of forces placing demands on the hospital.
2. *Internal analysis* – for each external force decide:
   (a) How is the hospital responding today?
   (b) What will happen if the hospital continues its present response?
   (c) What are the alternative responses?
3. *Issue identification and scenario analysis* – identify compatible and mutually exclusive alternatives; determine ideal responses not currently being demanded.
4. *Generation of alternatives and analysis of mission* – generate sets of alternative courses of action; determine core mission based on preferred courses of action.
5. *Creation of plan* – implement or move towards goals implied in core mission.
6. *Evaluation* – ongoing!

Based on Fry (1982).

## Poor quality of service

The following example illustrates the negative effects of poor service on one very influential customer.

### When service with a smile is missing by a mile

Why is it that supposedly excellent service organizations seem to slip up when my friends, family or I have dealings with them? If it were just because we are a pernickety lot, then we would presumably harbour the same complaint about the quality of products.

But we don't: in our experience, products with really good reputations generally seem to live up to their promise these days.

The reasons usually given for the patchy quality of most services relate to their supposed intangibility, and to their undoubtedly high reliance on that most fallible of factors, the human being. But there is more to the problem than that – as several supposed paragons need to recognize. Take Federal Express. The air courier company has become the subject of countless business school case studies on service excellence, and in 1990 it was the first leading service company to win America's Malcolm Baldridge National Quality Award.

Yet I have refused to use FedEx ever since the mid-1980s, when I was billed for months in error for a package sent from New York to London. To add insult to injury, the company sent its threatening letters from Paris, and in French! Neither its Paris office nor its UK counterpart ever acknowledged my desperate protestations to them.

Similar stories from a business acquaintance suggest that such problems arise not merely from the human errors of a few operatives, but from system design faults. . . .

Hertz car rental I shall avoid for ever – in America anyway – because of the chaos of its Boston airport operation one day in 1988, when a thrice-promised shuttle bus failed to show up, and I then had to queue for over an hour to collect a pre-booked car.

[The author then turns his attention to British Airways and three negative moments of truth he has experienced with them: the reduction in the number of ticket desks at Heathrow as an economy measure, thus creating long queues of angry passengers; an unanswered complaint about security lapses; and, worst of all, the meanness of its legroom on long-distance Economy Class flights.] Whereas BA's inadequate response to the security query was, one hopes, a single individual lapse from the normally prescribed level of service, the ticket desks and seating problems are both system faults: dubious economies in the design of products which form part of a service. . . . what are the lessons of these lapses?

First, that product and service quality are intertwined in intimate fashion. Quality service is not merely a question of getting one's front-line staff to behave impeccably in every one of their hundreds of daily customer contacts. . . .

Second, every aspect of the product and service must be designed, produced and delivered correctly – every time, and *ad infinitum*. As BA, and especially SAS have found, the people-intensity of a service makes its quality far harder to sustain than that of a product. . . . service companies must realize that as the pace of innovation quickens, and as many markets – such as airlines – become liberalized or simply more competitive – like retailing – last year's 'excellent' service may be this year's also-ran.

Underlying everything is the fact that customers who now demand a consistently high level of quality in products – even in low-priced ones – are starting to do the same in services. Such high expectations are fostered still further by the sort of hyperbolic advertising campaigns which service organizations, especially airlines, tend to run.  (Chris Lorenz, *Financial Times*, 10 January 1992)

Unfortunately for the firms concerned, the discontented client was an influential *Financial Times* journalist!

---

**Question**

How might the firms referred to rectify the problems that they are faced with?

---

### *'Over-servicing'*

One should also be wary of the dangers of 'over-servicing' as illustrated by the case of KwikFit, the tyre and exhaust service group – slogan 'You can't get better than a KwikFit fitter'. Their 'fast fit' servicing centres were criticized by the Consumer's Association in its magazine *Which?* because more than a quarter of forty-three KwikFit branches had recommended unnecessary work on a car brought in for a supposedly free inspection. Other fast service groups were rated as good or average according to whether or not they too recommended unnecessary work. Interestingly, this problem of moral hazard can arise in other forms of services. In medicine, for example, critics of private medicine, funded by individual insurance schemes, argue that this form of funding provides an incentive for doctors to provide unnecessary services, e.g. operations or drugs, hence the different rates, say, for appendectomies in Great Britain (low) and West Germany (high)!

## Strategic management and leadership

I didn't enjoy the job. I had to get rid of a lot of mates, and the way in which they left often made things worse – they were like Captain Oates, accepting the group need and sacrificing themselves – *Sir John Harvey-Jones, former chairman, talking about the pains of leadership at ICI.*

Strategic leadership requires . . . a readiness to discuss half-baked ideas, since most fully baked ideas start out in that form; a total honesty, a readiness to admit you got it wrong – *Sir John Hoskyns, former director general, Institute of Directors and executive chairman, Burton Group.*

Before talking about leadership it is worth making a few points about management. Studies of managers at work have focused on ten major roles in the management process (figure 5.5): interpersonal roles (figurehead, leader, liaison); informational roles (monitor, disseminator, spokesman); and decisional roles (entrepreneur, disturbance handler, resource allocator, negotiator).

The manager's key tasks are to design the work of his organization, to monitor its internal and external environment, to initiate change when necessary and to renew stability when faced with disturbance. How does the manager do this? How does he or she spend time? The classical

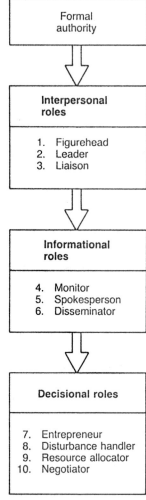

**Figure 5.5**   The manager's roles
*Source*: Mintzberg (1973)

management notion of the manager as a systematic, reflective, proactive planner has come to seem increasingly suspect. Managers are above all reactive, involved in scanning the environment for crucial information concerning their organizations, which they then need disseminate within that organization to manage it properly. The conventional wisdom that senior managers need aggregated information which can best be provided by a formal management information system is also suspect. Managers tend not to use this information even if available. They rely on meetings, often brief, and telephone calls, spending most of their time (more than 75 per cent in some cases) in verbal communication. Successful managers are likely to demonstrate a special ability to operate in peer relationships, to lead others in subordinate relationships, to resolve interpersonal and decisional conflicts, to deal in the verbal media, to make complex, interrelated decisions, to allocate resources (including their own time) and to innovate.

Key features of the managerial decision-making process are the splitting up of decisions (e.g. in the form of improvement projects), the sequencing of the ensuing steps, a concern with timing and the juggling of a number of projects. A prime managerial skill is the capacity to keep a number of issues in play over a long period of time until an appropriate moment arrives to activate one of them. Effective managers are those who gain control over their time in the sense that they are able to pick out and concentrate upon key issues in the plethora of demands made upon their time. An important element of time use is to ensure that they regularly communicate with colleagues and subordinates to share information and keep them in the picture. A key demand on the manager's time is the need to influence (rather than give orders). This necessity underlies the 'efficiency of seemingly inefficient behaviour' – in particular the fact that top managers do not plan their days in advance in much detail; they react – and their interactions tend to be short and disjointed. This has to be understood in the context of the generation and maintenance of agendas and networks in the pursuit of influence. Information networks, based on brief but frequent encounters, are of prime importance. They allow managers to disseminate their agendas for action and change.

Let us examine the manager's roles in more detail, starting with the *interpersonal*. As figurehead the manager serves as a symbol for the rest of the organization, a kind of role model demonstrating the corporate culture that he or she is responsible for creating. As leader he/she provides the sense of direction and purpose, exerts power to ensure staff have the necessary skills, and establishes mechanisms and processes so that he/she remains aware of what is happening in the organization. As liaisor the major role is to build a network of contacts between the organization and its external environment.

Next come the *informational* roles. As monitor the key tasks are to acquire information from as wide a variety of sources as possible and to shape this information into 'models' against which the organization can monitor its assessment of its environment, internal and external, and its performance. In the disseminator role the manager is responsible for sharing this information and the models within the organization. As spokesman (or spokeswoman) the manager is also responsible for 'sharing' this information externally in the best strategic way.

Two of the *decisional* roles are particularly important to the change process: those of entrepreneur and disturbance-handler. In the entrepreneur role the manager acts as initiator and designer of change, exploiting opportunities and solving non-urgent problems. He or she scans the environment, monitoring internal and external environments for opportunities and potential problems. He or she might, for example, question subordinates at random, hold review meetings, make unannounced tours of the organization. He or she develops, and 'juggles', a portfolio of improvement projects. As disturbance-handler the manager spends a great deal of time reacting very quickly to resolve disturbances, making changes because the moment demands them. Managerial processes are enormously complex and mysterious and rely on mental processes that we do not yet understand. These processes are more intuitive than intellectual. As resource allocator the key resource to be managed is the manager's own time, something the good manager seems to know how to do intuitively so that he/she concentrates on the key strategic issues. In this role he or she delegates but retains the power of final authorization before decisions are implemented. In the negotiator role the manager bargains with the various individuals and groups who have an interest or stake in strategic decisions.

Peters and Waterman were crucial in putting the subject of leadership at the centre of debates about strategic management. They sum up their views in the following words.

> Leadership is many things. It is patient, usually boring coalition building. It is purposeful seeding of cabals that one hopes will result in the appropriate ferment in the bowels of the organization. It is meticulously shifting the attention of the institution through the mundane language of management systems. It is altering agendas so that new priorities get enough attention. It is being visible when things are going wrong and invisible when they are working well. It's building a loyal team at the top that speaks more or less with one

voice. It's listening carefully much of the time, frequently speaking with encouragement, and reinforcing words with believable action. It's being tough when necessary, and it's the occasional naked use of power or the 'subtle accumulation of nuances, a hundred things done a little better'.  (Peters and Waterman: 1982: 82)

It has been said of British industry that it is overmanaged and 'underled'. Leaders do intangible things like define a mission, express a vision, inspire their employees and provoke change. There are two essential preconditions for change. Significant people need to feel there is a need for change. They then have to convince others of this need before meaningful, lasting change can occur. The need for it must be felt throughout the organization. A key leadership task is motivating. Peters and Waterman argue that managers in excellent companies are adept at motivating by compelling, simple – even beautiful – values. These managers demonstrate 'transforming leadership' – leadership 'that builds on man's need for meaning [and] creates institutional purpose'. They induce clarity, consensus and commitment regarding the organization's basic purposes. The key role of the chief executive is to manage the *values* of the organization.

Chester Barnard, a seminal figure in management, highlighted what he saw as three main executive functions: (i) to provide the system of communication; (ii) to promote essential effort; and (iii) to formulate and define purpose. The latter function equates with setting the strategic vision/mission of the organization. A fast-changing, complex environment places a premium on leadership which gives greater attention to the role, mission, philosophy and overall culture of the organization. The major defaults of leadership are failure to set goals and setting goals that only enjoy superficial acceptance. A strategy needs to be acceptable and to challenge, motivate and excite.

Management has traditionally been concerned with performance, the organization's ability to accomplish its goals. Leadership is concerned with the organization's mission and culture. The main management leadership goal should be the creation of a common culture of shared values geared to the accomplishment of a common goal. Management and leadership come together to the extent that good managers keep themselves well informed with what is happening in their organization, keep what they consider the key interests of the organization alive, ultimately focusing their time and energy on a limited number of key issues. Managers play the power game, effectively knowing where they can mobilize support and how to deflate opposition, and know how to satisfy the organization that it has a sense of direction.

*Leaders on leadership*

The enterprise required of innovating managers . . . is not the creative spark of genius that invents a new idea, but rather the skill with which they move outside the formal bonds of their job, manoeuvring through and around the organization in sometimes risky, unique and novel ways. This is what the corporate entrepreneur has in common with the classic definition of an entrepreneur. Organizational genius is 10 percent inspiration and 90 acquisition – acquisition of power to move beyond a formal job charter and to influence others – *Rosabeth Kanter, editor of the* Harvard Business Review.

Successful leaders take actions which help achieve tasks, help build *esprit de corps* and help motivate individuals. All the leader's tasks arise from these basic functions; plan schedule; assess team; explain roles; monitor progress; support efforts; evaluate results; and debrief – *Chris Bonington, perhaps Britain's most successful mountaineer, certainly the most famous.*

---

## Questions

1. Are you happy with the distinction between managers and leaders?
2. Have you worked with or for anybody you consider a good leader? If *yes*, what qualities did he or she have?
3. Why is good leadership important?
4. Are leaders born or made?
5. Chris Bonington has also said that the leader and the team must find the right balance. What do you think he means by this?

---

## Exhibit 5.2   Leaders in action – I

### Jan Carlsson and SAS

Jan Carlsson became president of SAS (Scandinavian Airlines Systems) at a time when the airline was struggling in the early 1980s. Under his leadership the company went from a loss to a profit of $71m on sales of $2bn in just over a year. His work at SAS provides an exemplar of how to compete in service quality. His focus on strategic change at SAS was more on process and organizational structure than on products. He did develop Euroclass, SAS's version of business class, but more important was his thinking on the nature of service and the type of organization needed to deliver it in a way that satisfied the customer and brought repeat business, thus producing turnaround in his company. His approach is described in his autobiography, *Moments of Truth*. In this book he describes his role not as fount of all knowledge and omniscient decision-maker, but as facilitator of the best possible decisions by improving the decision-making process and organizational structure: 'The company was not asking me to make all the decisions on my own, only to create the right atmosphere, the right conditions for others to do their jobs better.' He appealed to his employees, involving them in the process of change: 'You are the ones who must help me, not the other way around!' He gave his employees the authority and responsibility to act, making frontline workers, particularly travel agents and stewards and stewardesses, into managers, giving them the authority to 'respond to the needs and problems of individual customers'. Middle managers were no longer to be supervisors but resources to help the frontline workers.

With Carlsson at the helm SAS was voted 'airline of the year' as a result of its efforts to improve its service 'by putting the customer first'. His great achievement was to create awareness of and enthusiasm for the concept of service at every level and in every location in an organization employing 20,000. He did this by a combination of visionary leadership, exceptional powers of communication and intensive training programmes (Sadler, 1988). He convinced his employees that they were responsible for the quality of the '50,000 moments of truth' that the company had to face each and every day. Moments of truth in service are the often fleeting encounters between employees and customers, where the customer senses he or she is truly being served. On their quality depends the customer's impression of the organization. These encounters render the notion of service into a tangible experience that the customers carry away with them. Carlsson's key task was to convince his employees of the strategic importance of embracing this existential approach of service as a competitive edge in the hostile environment of airline competition.

*Question*: Is Carlsson's approach applicable to other organizations?

## Exhibit 5.3   Leaders in action – II

### Sir John Harvey-Jones – making it happen

Sir John's views on the qualities necessary for good management and leadership can be summed up as follows:

1.  *A determination to be the best*. In his case to create the best chemical company in the world.
2.  *Patience*. The knowledge that such an objective can only be achieved by solidly and carefully building a new company culture.
3.  *Breadth of vision*. His idea of 'best' did not just embrace profitability. His vision of the best company included being the best in bringing in new products; in market sensitivity; presence; range; quality; how the company dealt with people; ethical, environmental and safety standards.
4.  *Taking the long-term view*. Seeing his success or failure as judged by where the company would be five years later.
5.  *A leader, rather than a manager*. Leading by example and persuasion, and hard work, not on the basis of power or authority. Being able to help others release their energies and focus their efforts on corporate objectives; creating conditions in which people want to give of their best.
6.  *Humility*. Detesting 'red carpet' treatment, subservience, hierarchy and flattery. Being willing to own up to making mistakes.
7.  *Openness*. Trying to make ICI a more open and friendly organization and one in which constructive criticism of top management is accepted.
8.  *Compassion*. During his years of office ICI shed 60,000 jobs – something he genuinely feels sad about.

*Source*: Sadler (1988: 139).

*Question*: How would you rank order these eight qualities?

## Corporate responsibility

It is fitting to end a book on strategic management with a consideration of corporate responsibility, a subject that is increasingly demanding the attention of top management. One of the earliest and most influential models of the strategic management decision process, the Harvard 'Design School' model, suggested that the basic building blocks of strategy encompass four factors: (i) an organization's strengths and weaknesses; (ii) opportunities and threats in its environment; (iii) the values of its managers; and (iv) its broader social responsibility. Most attention in strategic management has been paid to the analysis of internal and external factors. We have suggested in chapters 4 and 5 that the values of top managers are also a crucial determinant of strategy. We also suggest in our model of strategic management (figure 1.1) that one has to balance the interests of various stakeholders in taking strategic decisions. The broad notion of stakeholders encompasses a range of parties that determine what is in the broader societal interest.

The first issue in corporate responsibility is that of 'private solutions to public problems'. The arguments concern corporate responsibility for aspects of social welfare that the state cannot or will not provide. In this context business is increasingly expected to be responsive to the needs of the community and society. It is not enough for companies only to be concerned with the needs of shareholders and employees. This view is most developed and accepted in the United States but one of the themes of Thatcherism in the United Kingdom in the 1980s was that the state expected business leaders to help in the revitalization of the economy of inner cities. Businesses were urged to look on this as an investment, providing returns in terms of good public relations and in providing an edge in recruiting the best local labour. Out of this approach came initiatives such as 'Business in the Community'.

The second dominant theme in corporate responsibility is that of business ethics and the claim that ethical decision-making is a business as well as a moral imperative. Equal opportunities is a case in point. Also, investment decisions are increasingly examined in an ethical light. Ethical investment trusts appear to have performed above the average in the latter part of the 1980s. Green issues and industrial disasters have heightened moral concern. Only ethical management, the strong proponents of this argument suggest, will survive and prosper in an increasingly ethical world. In her autobiography *Body and Soul*, Anita Roddick, founder of Body Shop, a major UK success of the 1980s, tells of her search for 'the modern-day equivalent of those Quakers who ran successful businesses, made money because they offered honest products and treated their people decently, worked hard, spent honestly, gave honest value for money, put back more than they took out and told no lies', only to conclude that 'This business creed, sadly, seems long forgotten.' Ms Roddick set out to 'remoralize' an industry that, she claimed, had absolutely no sense of moral responsibility and went as far as to claim that by the turn of the millennium any company that does not operate in the same ethical way as the Body Shop will risk failure. Sir Adrian Cadbury makes a similar point about the effect of insider trading scandals on the junk bond market in the United States. It is not just the companies associated with such scandals that have been damaged, but the entire industry.

The importance of corporate responsibility, broadly defined, to strategy can be illustrated in three hypotheses:

- *The stakeholder hypothesis* – Organizations are stronger to the extent that they demonstrate a broad sense of responsibility to a variety of stakeholders, both external and internal. The Japanese *kaisha* provides a potent illustration of the importance of management accepting responsibility for internal stakeholders.
- *The vision hypothesis* – 'Visionary' organizations whose missions capitalize on emerging social trends have been among the success stories of the 1970s and 1980s, e.g. Body Shop with its new vision of the cosmetic industry as socially responsible.
- *The value hypothesis* – The values of top managers have a crucial role to play in the strategic management process. The extent to which these values are 'responsible' will increasingly impact upon the fate of the organization. The study of corporate responsibility and business ethics have important roles to play in the surfacing of core values and their clarification. One should also be aware, however, of the ambiguity of supposedly responsible and irresponsible behaviours.

### Stakeholders

The term stakeholder refers to any group or individual who has a legitimate expectation of a firm. Stakeholders include stockholders, employees, customers, suppliers, creditors, managers, local community, special interest groups such as environmentalists, the general public, government and any other groups who have entered into relationships with the firm. A stakeholder map of a large organization is set out in figure 5.6.

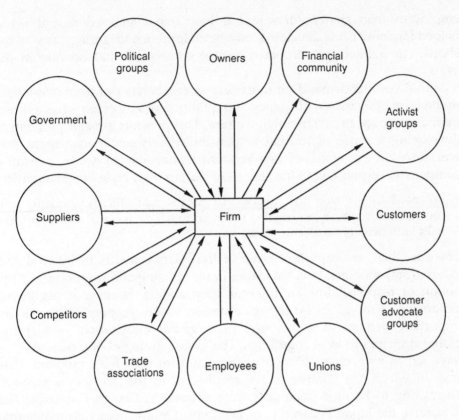

**Figure 5.6**  Stakeholder map of a very large organization
*Source*: Freeman (1984)

Such a map provides an image of stakeholder groups. It thus illustrates graphically the range of stakeholders the corporation is responsible to and needs to seek to satisfy. The emphasis on stakeholders also suggests that Porter's five-forces model of industrial structure needs to be extended to embrace the relative power of those stakeholders that Porter's five forces do not accommodate.

The implication of the stakeholder approach is that organizations must ask themselves searching questions about the range of their stakeholders and their relative power. In firms such as Ford one can construe major changes in management style and corporate ethic as, in part, a redefinition of the corporation's responsibility to its employees and other stakeholders. Here Japanese management practices have played an important role in changing accepted managerial wisdom in the West. Japanese strategic management seems more orientated to the maximization of the interests of employees than shareholders and it has been suggested that this has helped Japanese firms develop a long-term approach to strategy, free of the short-term market for corporate control constraints that operate in the West.

In the West the demand for more responsible behaviour from employees in the form of increased efficiency and quality is often perceived as a threat by the employee to his/her own welfare. This presents a major problem in developing a sense of mutual responsibility between management and workforce. In the words of one Western manager from Xerox, a leading company in responding to the lessons of the Japanese style of management:

> We need to get over the hurdle that means that efficiency, quality and competence results in loss of jobs. You need to have a sense of security to take risks with new jobs and new skills.

There is, then, an important issue of the relative merits of internal and external stakeholders. Japan, a leader in recognizing and responding to the notion of responsibility for internal stakeholders, is now, in its global expansion strategies, targeting broader social responsibility as an important element of what Sony calls 'global localization' – adapting global strategies to local conditions. The global strategies of Japanese firms have led to investment friction in the countries they have targeted. One way in which the Japanese have responded to this friction is through attempting to become good corporate citizens in foreign countries. The *Keidanren*, the Japan Federation of Economic Organizations estimates that US corporate donations amount to about 2 per cent of gross national product. In Japan the figure is a mere 0.1 percent. However, in Japan the concept of corporate responsibility includes such things as job security (for core workers), import promotion and price stability.

## Visionary organizations

The strategy literature has paid increasing attention to 'organizational vision'. 'Visionary' organizations whose missions capitalize on emerging social trends have been among the success stories of the 1970s and 1980s. Body Shop, with its new vision of the cosmetic industry as socially responsible, has already been mentioned. Apple, with its vision of democratizing the computer industry by bringing computer power to the people, springs to mind. At the turn of the century Henry Ford's vision of democratizing the automobile industry led to mass production. Other visions focus on internal transformation. The 'Aspirations Statement' of Levi-Strauss begins: 'We all want a company that our people are proud of and committed to, where all employees have an opportunity to contribute, learn, grow and advance based on merit, not politics or background.'

Mission statements increasingly refer to a broad range of stakeholders. Ford's statement of Mission, Values and Guiding Principles (figure 1.6) includes a clear commitment to stockholders, the owners of the business, employees, dealers and suppliers, as well as to a broader social responsibility. This represents a broadening of their responsibility agenda, particularly in the area of internal stakeholders, driven by a reanalysis and redefinition of their core values. It is the combination of mission, vision and values that can create the common identity necessary to unite the large number of people that constitute a large organization. Peter Senge emphasizes the importance of shared vision as a key aspect of the learning organization. The impetus to learning is to foster an environment in which people share their visions of the organization, and through this process of sharing create a common future. Through the creation of a common vision organizations can overcome the sectionalism that is inimical to the sense of shared responsibility for the organization's fate.

> Getting started is as simple as sitting people in small circles and asking them to talk about 'what's really important to them'.... When people begin to state and hear each other's visions, the foundation of the political environment begins to crumble – the belief that all we care about is self-interest. Organizations that fail to foster genuinely shared visions, or that foist unilateral visions on their members and pretend that they are shared, fail to tap this broader commitment. Though they decry internal politics, they do nothing to nurture a nonpolitical environment.

It is only in a non-political environment that responsibility for the common good can be generated. 'One of the deepest desires underlying shared vision is the desire to be connected, to a larger purpose *and* one another. The spirit of connection is fragile' (Senge, 1990: 275).

## Values

Chester Barnard taught us that a primary role of senior management is the fostering of shared values in the organization. The Ford example illustrates how major strategic change necessitates a fundamental re-examination of the organization's value-system. At Ford the re-examination of values came before the framing of the mission and the guiding principles and, indeed, was a necessary precursor to the later initiatives. Strategic change focused on the need for better-quality products to compete with Japanese automobile firms. The key to unlocking the potential to manufacture to this quality was the redefinition of the value of people to the organization. Strategic management, Ford was accepting, needs to be responsible management.

---

### Exhibit 5.4   Body Shop

Anita Roddick has created a business empire through the espousal of a new sense of business mission. Central to her concerns is an ethical approach to business, for example, in the areas of animal testing of products and 'green' environmental issues. Not a single decision is taken in the company without considering environmental and social issues. Her approach to business is summed up by the following principles:

- no advertising;
- minimize packaging;
- emphasis on health rather than beauty;
- no wild claims about products;
- recruiting policy;
- equality of working conditions for all staff;
- profit sharing;
- working for and with the community;
- franchising;
- no diversification/no acquisitions.

*Source*: MBA project, University of Nottingham.

---

Body Shop is one of the great business success stories of our times, yet it is not without its critics who, for example, contest the claims about animal testing, criticize franchising as favouring the company at the expense of the franchisee, argue that it is unethical to use ethics as a promotion device, and claim that the company might not spend money on advertising but that it is very adept at promoting media attention, a form of covert advertising, usually focused on Ms Roddick herself.

## Question

Anita Roddick is a woman with a burning social purpose. She is championing a new philosophy of retailing, illustrated by the following quotations:

I think loneliness is a time bomb ticking away in our society, especially in the shopping malls. Anyone who can figure a way of reducing loneliness, either through their stores or their marketing, will have a business that will thrive for ever.

Never treat customers as enemies, approach them as potential friends.

Think of customers as guests, make them laugh.

Is any retailer thinking about how to make a shopping mall function socially as an arena of human contact or centre for useful, social information, like a village well in traditional societies? I doubt it.

She claims that her ethical approach to business will become the norm for the twenty-first century. Do you agree with her views and the Body Shop approach or do you count yourself as one of its critics?

## Epilogue

Strategic management, then, is about responsible management. In the final analysis, the 'buck stops' with those managers who are empowered to sanction the critical strategic decisions that will, in the long-term, make or break a company. This is a heavy weight for managers to bear. We wish you well!

## Final word

*Sir John Harvey-Jones on his 'retirement'*: 'I never gave ICI a backward glance. I was knackered.'

# Further reading

Readers interested in exploring the issues in strategic management beyond the level and scope of the present text, or simply for an alternative perspective, may find the following useful:

Asch, D. and Bowman, C. 1989: *Readings in Strategic Management*. London: Macmillan, 1989.

Bartlett, C. A. and Ghoshal, S. C. 1989: *Managing Across Borders*. London: Hutchinson Business Books.

Bowman, C. 1990: *The Essence of Strategic Management*. London: Prentice Hall.

Hickman, C. R. and Silva, M. 1985: *Creating Excellence: merging corporate cultures, strategy and change in the new age*. London: Allen & Unwin.

Johnson, G. and Scholes, K. 1988: *Exploring Corporate Strategy*, 2nd edn. London: Prentice Hall.

Mintzberg, H. and Quinn, J. B. 1991: *The Strategy Process*, 2nd edn. New York: Prentice Hall.

Morgan, G. 1986: *Images of Organization*. Beverly Hills, Calif.: Sage.

Morgan, G. 1989: *Creative Organization Theory*. Beverly Hills, Calif.: Sage.

Morita, A. 1987: *Made in Japan*. London: Fontana.

Pascale, R. T. 1990: *Managing on the Edge*. New York: Viking.

Peters, T. and Waterman, R. H. 1982: *In Search of Excellence*. New York: Harper & Row.

Pettigrew, A. M. 1985: *The Awakening Giant: continuity and change in ICI*. Oxford: Blackwell.

Porter, M. 1980: *Competitive Strategy*. New York: Free Press.

Porter, M. 1985: *Competitive Advantage*. New York: Free Press.

Sadler, P. 1988: *Managerial Leadership in the Post-Industrial Society*. Aldershot: Gower.

Senge, P. 1990: *The Fifth Dimension*. New York: Doubleday, 1990.

# References

Abernathy, W. J., Clark, K. and Kantrow, A. 1981: The new industrial competition. *Harvard Business Review*, September–October, pp. 68–81.

Ansoff, I. 1965: *Corporate Strategy*. New York: McGraw-Hill.

Barnard, C. I. 1938: *The Functions of the Executive*. Boston, Mass.: Harvard University Press.

Bartlett, C. A. and Ghoshal, S. 1989: *Managing Across Borders*. London: Hutchinson Business Books.

Barnatt, C. and Starkey, K. 1991: The case for flexibility: a study of the UK television industry. Working Paper, School of Management and Finance, University of Nottingham.

Best, M. H. 1990: *The New Competition*. Oxford: Polity Press.

Cadbury, A. 1991: Business strategy. Esmee Fairbairn Distinguished Lecture Series, Inaugural Lecture, Lancaster University, 7 November.

Carlsson, J. 1989: *Moments of Truth*. New York: Harper & Row.

Cronshaw, M., Davis, E. and Kay, J. 1990: On being stuck in the middle or good food costs less at Sainsbury's. Working Paper no. 83, Centre for Business Strategy, London Business School.

David, F. R. 1989: How companies define their mission. *Long Range Planning*, 22, 90–7.

Davidson, I. and Mallin, C. 1993: *The Business Accounting and Finance Blueprint*. Oxford: Blackwell.

Ennew, C. 1993: *The Marketing Blueprint*. Oxford: Blackwell.

Ennew, C., Watkins, T. and Wright, M. 1990: *Marketing Financial Services*. London: Heinemann.

Freeman, R. H. 1984: *Strategic Management: a stakeholder approach*. London: Pitman.

Fry, R. E. 1982: Improving trustee, administrator and physician collaboration through open systems planning. In N. Margulies and J. D. Adams (eds), *Organizational Development in Health Care Organizations*. Reading, Mass.: Addison-Wesley.

Galbraith, J. R. and Kazanjian, R. K. 1986: *Strategy Implementation*. St Paul, Minn.: West Publishing.

Hamel, G. and Prahalad, C. K. 1989: Strategic intent. *Harvard Business Review*, May–June, pp. 63–76.

Harvey-Jones, J. 1988: *Making It Happen*. London: Collins.

Hickman, C. R. and Silva, M. 1985: *Creating Excellence: merging corporate cultures, strategy and change in the new age*. London: Allen & Unwin.

Johnson, G. and Scholes, K. 1988: *Exploring Corporate Strategy*, 2nd edn. New York: Prentice Hall.

Knee, D. and Walters, D. 1985: *Strategy in Retailing*. Oxford: Philip Allen.

Lanzilloti, R. F. 1961: The automobile industry. In W. Adams (ed.), *Structure of American Industry*, 3rd edn. London: Macmillan.

Miles, R. E. and Snow, C. 1986: Organizations: new concepts for new forms. *California Management Review*, 28(3), 62–73.

Mintzberg, H. 1973: *The Nature of Managerial Work*. New York: Harper & Row.

Morgan, G. 1986: *Images of Organization*. Beverly Hills, Calif.: Sage.

Morgan, G. 1989: *Creative Organization Theory*. Beverly Hills, Calif.: Sage.

Morita, A. 1987: *Made in Japan*. London: Fontana.

Naylor, T., Vernon, J. and Wertz, K. 1983: *Managerial Economics: corporate economics and strategy*. New York: McGraw-Hill.

Ouchi, W. G. 1981: *Theory Z: how American business can meet the Japanese challenge*. Reading, Mass.: Addison-Wesley.

Pascale, R. T. 1990: *Managing on the Edge*. New York: Viking.

Peters, T. and Waterman, R. H. 1982: *In Search of Excellence*. New York: Harper & Row.

Pettigrew, A. M. 1985: *The Awakening Giant: continuity and change in ICI*. Oxford: Blackwell.

Pilkington, J. R. A. 1991: A study of strategy formulation in an automotive manufacturer. Unpublished Ph.D. thesis, University of Aston, Birmingham.

Porter, M. E. 1979: How competitive forces shape strategy. *Harvard Business Review*, March–April, pp. 137–45.

Porter, M. E. 1980: *Competitive Strategy: techniques for analyzing industries and competitors*. New York: The Free Press.

Porter, M. E. 1985: *Competitive Advantage: creating and sustaining superior performance*. New York: The Free Press.

Porter, M. E. 1990: *The Competitive Advantage of Nations*. New York: The Free Press.

Pucik, V. and Hatvany, N. 1983: Management practices in Japan and their impact on business strategy. *Advances in Strategic Management*, vol. 1, JAI Press.

Quinn, J. B. 1980: *Strategy for Change: logical incrementalism*. Homewood, Ill.: Irwin.

Quinn, J. B., Mintzberg, H. and James, R. 1988: *The Strategy Process*. Englewood Cliffs, NJ: Prentice Hall.

Roddick, A. 1991: *Body and Soul*. London: Ebury Press.

Sadler, P. 1988: *Managerial Leadership in the Post-Industrial Society*. Aldershot: Gower.

Scherer, F. M. and Ross, D. 1989: *Industrial Market Structure and Economic Performance*, 3rd edn. Boston, Mass.: Houghton Mifflin.

Seeger, J. A. 1984: Reversing the images of BCG's growth share matrix. *Strategic Management Journal*.

Senge, P. 1990: *The Fifth Dimension*. New York: Doubleday.

Singh, S., Utton, M. and Waterson, M. 1991a: An introduction and a pen portrait of the whole sample by industry. Discussion Papers in Industrial Economics, no. 27, Department of Economics, University of Reading.

Singh, S., Utton, M. and Waterson, M. 1991b: Entry deterring strategies by established firms. Discussion Papers in Industrial Economics, no. 28, Department of Economics, University of Reading.

Smiley, R. 1988: 'Empirical evidence on strategic entry deterrence. *International Journal of Industrial Organization*, 6, 167–80.

Thompson, A. A. 1989: *The Economics of the Firm*, 5th edn. New York: Prentice Hall.

Tse, K. K. 1985: *Marks & Spencer*. Oxford: Pergamon Press.

# Index

## Business Blueprints

The following titles are available in this practical new series:

Christine Ennew: *The Marketing Blueprint*   0 631 18715 4   ☐
Paul Dobson: *The Strategic Management Blueprint*   0 631 18624 7   ☐
Ian Davidson: *The Business Accounting and Finance Blueprint*
   0 631 18687 5   ☐

All titles are £11.99 each.

You can order through your local bookseller or, in case of difficulty, direct from the publisher using this order form. Please indicate the quantity of books you require in the boxes above and complete the details on the form below.

**Payment**
Please add £2.50 to payment to cover p&p.

☐ Please charge my Mastercard/Visa/American Express account card
   number ☐☐☐☐☐☐☐☐☐☐☐☐☐☐☐☐☐☐

Expiry date _____

Signature _____
         (credit card orders must be signed to be valid)

☐ I enclose a cheque for £_____ made payable to **Marston Book Services Ltd**

   (PLEASE PRINT)

Name _____

Address _____

_____

_____ Postcode _____

Tel No _____

Signature _____ Date _____

Please return the completed form with remittance to:
**Business Direct, Blackwell Publishers, 108 Cowley Road, Oxford OX4 1JF, UK
or Fax your credit card order to Oxford (0865) 791347 (Attn Business Direct) or Telephone your credit card order to Oxford (0865) 791100 (Attn Business Direct).**

Goods will be despatched within 14 days of receipt of order. Data supplied may be used to inform you about other Basil Blackwell publications in relevant fields.
Registered in England No. 180277 Basil Blackwell Ltd.